Introduction

All the activities in this book have, as their focus, 'patterns' which come from differen
surrounds us in both the natural and man-made world - we wear it, sit on it, eat off it a..u v.,......
uses pattern in a variety of ways and for a variety of purposes. Some patterns are decorative and ornamental, others
are traditional or have a religious or cultural significance e.g. status.

Throughout history patterns have been used as symbols and motifs and in specific colours to convey meaning, deliver
messages and ensure continuity. I have included a little background information to accompany each pattern i.e. where
it comes from, who would use it / wear it and its significance to each culture.

The techniques used to produce patterns vary throughout the world e.g. they can be printed, dyed, drawn, woven,
painted, embossed, rubbed, stitched, impressed, collaged, carved etc. and I have incorporated many of these different
techniques throughout the book.

The materials in and on which patterns are produced also vary hence I have included a range of different materials to
be used for the activities e.g. paper, card, clay, etc. They are only suggestions and teachers may want to choose and
use different ones.

The activities naturally have strong links with other areas of the Curriculum e.g. History, Geography, Maths, ICT etc. as
well as Art and Design, thus making them an integral part of the 'Creative Curriculum', appropriate for pupils in both Key
Stage One and Key Stage Two.

Each activity lists the equipment needed, includes a 'talk about' section, a 'doing' section and gives ideas for display.

I have greatly enjoyed researching this book and hope you too will enjoy exploring the world of pattern contained within
it. Hopefully it will lead both you and the children in your class to discover and investigate even more patterns from parts
of the globe that are not included here.

Dianne Williams

Many thanks to
Gail Bonney Loans Officer Lancashire County Museum Education
Alison McClay Teacher Adviser for Ethnic Minority Achievement
for their help and support in the writing of this book.

Step by Step Art Books are available from all good Educational Bookshops and by mail order from:
Topical Resources, P.O. Box 329, Broughton, Preston, Lancashire. PR3 5LT
Topical Resources publishes a range of Educational Materials for use in Primary Schools and Pre-School Nurseries and Playgroups.

For the latest catalogue
Tel 01772 863158 / Fax 01772 866153
e.mail: sales@topical-resources.co.uk
Visit our Website at: www.topical-resources.co.uk

Copyright © 2008 Dianne Williams

Designed by Paul Sealey Design Services, 3 Wentworth Drive, Thornton, Lancashire.

First Published September 2008.
ISBN: 978-1-905509-73-7

Contents

Tartan

Tartan is a chequered pattern that has been used in weaving for centuries. The colours, and the sequence in which they are used, identify individual clans and give a sense of belonging to groups of people who are in some way related e.g. the British Royal family uses the Royal Stewart tartan because of their ancestral links to James IV of Scotland. Today new tartans are invented and registered every year. As well as Scottish tartans there are Canadian tartans, American tartans (plaid), Northern English tartans, Welsh tartans and Cornish tartans.

Equipment Needed

Squares of sugar paper in assorted colours (16 x 16 cm approx.), thick and thin strips of sugar paper in assorted colours, glue, scissors and examples of several different tartan patterns.

Talk About

*   Where the countries that favour tartan are found on a world map and on a map of the British Isles.
*   Finding examples of tartan patterns from these different countries on the Internet.
*   The way the lines are arranged to form a tartan pattern - across each other, next to each other, over and under each other plus the different thicknesses of the lines. Ask the children to touch and follow different lines in a pattern.
*   The number of colours used in each of the examples of tartan.
*   Arranging strips of paper on a coloured square to make a tartan pattern.
*   Where to put the glue to stick the pattern down and how much glue to use.
*   How to trim the strips if they extend over the edges of the square (turn the square over once the strips have been stuck down to make it easy to cut off any extra bits).

Doing

*   Decide on the colour scheme you are going to use for your pattern and choose a selection of thick and thin strips that match it plus a square of coloured paper as the background.

*   Arrange the strips across and up and down the background square to make a tartan pattern – you may need to get more strips to complete your pattern. Remember the same colours must be repeated in the same sequence throughout. You may need to try several arrangements before you have the pattern you want to keep.
*   Get some glue and carefully stick your pattern down then trim off any strips that extend over the edge of the background.

Display

Put examples of actual tartan patterns in the centre of the display board plus information about tartan and the names of some of the different tartans. Arrange the children's work around the edge of this, each piece touching the one next to it. Leave the work unmounted and add a plain border around the edge of the board.

Fair Isle

The Shetland Isles to the north of Scotland are renowned for their brightly coloured, patterned knitwear. The patterns are made up of rows of geometrical and symmetrical motifs - often similar to snowflakes. It was common for a grandmother to knit the first sweater for her grandson when he reached adolescence - his Robe of Glory. This would be patterned throughout e.g. with the Water of Life, the Seed of Life, the Flower of Life, the Anchor of Hope plus Star patterns to guide him on his way. The shoulders would be decorated with the Crown of Glory pattern as the ultimate reward for a good life.

Equipment Needed

'Dot Lattice' grid maths paper, coloured felt tip pens, drawing pencils (4B - 6B), rulers, pictures and examples of Fair Isle patterns, geometric shapes and snow flake designs from old Christmas cards.

Talk About

- Where the Shetland Isles are plus pictures and examples of Fair Isle patterns and snowflake designs.
- What geometrical motifs are and finding one in a Fair Isle pattern. What symmetrical means and finding a symmetrical motif in a Fair Isle Pattern.
- How the same motifs are repeated - often in rows in the same colour - to make up a pattern and how they fit together.
- Drawing geometric shapes using a pencil and ruler on the dot lattice grid paper by joining up the dots in different ways.
- Using these shapes to make a repeating pattern along a line.
- Filling in and outlining these shapes using felt tip pens, remembering to use the same colours for the shapes that are identical and match.

Doing

- Tell the children to draw a horizontal line with a pencil and a ruler across the dot lattice grid, leaving space above and below it.
- They now need to decide which geometric shapes they are going to use to make up their pattern. Suggest they limit the number of shapes to 2 or 3 to make it easy to repeat them.
- Once they have drawn the outline of their shapes in a repeating pattern, suggest they look at them and perhaps add smaller shapes within the large ones or lines for additional decoration. Remind them that these must be repeated in sequence.
- Using felt tip pens, the children need to fill in their shapes remembering (again) to use the same colours for each of the matching shapes and lines. Finally outline the shapes if required, using a ruler to help neaten the edges.

Display

Cut out the silhouette of a jumper in black and put it in the middle of the board. Write information about Fair Isle patterns and put this on the silhouette. Arrange the children's designs, individually mounted, in rows around the edge.

Aran Patterns

Off the west coast of Ireland is the Isle of Aran noted for knitwear designs that feature cables, twists and bobbles in natural cream wool. Such designs are said to represent the fisherman's life and the environment (nets, waves, rocks etc.) in which he lives and works. The wife of a newly married fisherman would knit a sweater to keep him warm and dry during his working day. This would have a central panel, which would become the basis of a family design. When a son was born, a different panel would be added either side of the family panel - each additional son would have his own design alongside the family panel as would grandchildren. A family could thus be identified by the central panel, common to all its members, and its branches by the patterns on either side.

Equipment Needed

Black paper A4 size and pieces of scrap paper, pencils, white and yellow paint, paintbrushes and pieces of card to use as palettes; examples of Aran patterns from knitting patterns and the Internet.

Talk About

- Where the Isle of Aran is and the examples of Aran patterns.
- What cables, bobbles and diamonds are and finding them in the patterns.
- How these shapes are arranged in columns that are often repeated in the design.
- Mixing cream coloured paint by combining a little yellow and a lot of white.
- Drawing lines and curves using a paintbrush and dabbing with a paintbrush to produce bobbles.
- Drawing a pattern of lines, diamonds and bobbles in pencil on a piece of scrap paper.

Doing

- The children try out various combinations of cables, twists, diamonds and bobbles, in pencil on scrap paper to create a preferred sketch.
- The children need to choose a piece of A4 black paper and arrange in portrait form on the surface in front of them.
- With a finger they could draw cables, twists, diamonds and bobbles, on their paper to judge how big they need to be to fill the paper.
- Using a pencil sketch for reference, they now need to copy their design using a paintbrush and cream paint onto to their black paper.

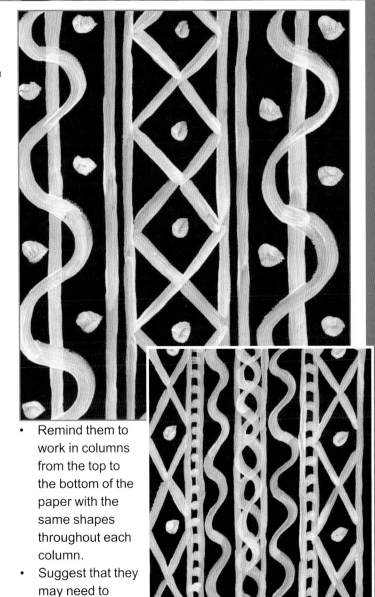

- Remind them to work in columns from the top to the bottom of the paper with the same shapes throughout each column.
- Suggest that they may need to repeat the same lines and shapes more than once to fill their paper.
- Similar patterns could be made in relief on a clay tile and texture and interest added by pressing in reclaimed materials e.g. straws, pegs etc.

Display

The completed pieces of work could be arranged un-mounted as a block, each piece touching its neighbour in the middle of the board. This could be surrounded by 'cut out' and real knitting needles plus knitting terms copied from knitting patterns and typed up using the computer.

Canal Boat Decorations

Canal boats, or 'narrow boats', and the every day items on them e.g. buckets, water barrels, water jugs, stools etc. are often highly decorated with colourful folk art. This originated when the canals were built during the industrial revolution. Traditional motifs were roses, leaves, daisies, castles, stripes and playing card symbols (hearts, clubs and diamonds for good luck) in bright shades of white, yellow, red, black and green. They appear usually on a background of dark bottle green or black. Colourful name plates complete the decoration. Most of the painting was done by the boat builders rather than professional artists.

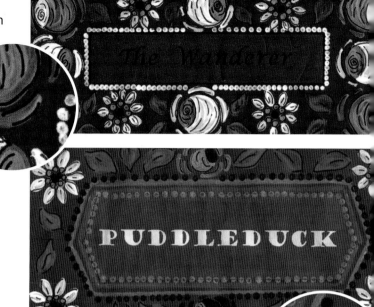

Equipment Needed

Paint in bright shades of red, yellow and green plus black and white. Pieces of card to use as palettes, paint brushes, pieces of scrap paper and drawing pencils (4B-6B). Scissors, letter templates, pieces (A3 size approx.) and broad strips of dark green and red paper plus examples of the type of traditional decorations found on canal boats.

Talk About

- The development of narrow boats for canal transport and as homes for the people who worked on them.
- The colours and shapes found in narrow boat decoration and the names of each type of decoration.
- The sort of utensils that were decorated and what they were used for.
- The type of names found on the boats and how they were decorated i.e. in brightly coloured letters surrounded by border patterns.
- Choosing a name (of their own) for a narrow boat.
- Drawing a utensil (to decorate) for a narrow boat.
- Sketching a design in pencil on scrap paper and carefully copying the shapes used in traditional decorations. Drawing these shapes on scrap paper with a paint brush before adding them to their final work.

Doing

- Ask the children to choose to make either a decorated name plate for a boat or a utensil to go on it and to sketch their design in pencil on a scrap piece of paper. When they are happy with their design they need to choose the paper for their final work - a broad strip for a name plate - an A3 piece for a utensil.
- For a name plate they will need to use the letter templates or the computer to write the name across the middle of the strip leaving a border around the edge for further decoration. For a utensil e.g. a bucket, they will need to draw its outline shape nearly as big as the A3 paper before cutting it out.
- Finally they need to put the colours of paint they will use on to a card palette and with a paintbrush begin to draw and then fill in the shapes to complete their design. They can use their pencil sketches for reference.

Display

Arrange the nameplates around the edge of the board as a border. Cut out the silhouette of a narrow boat in black to go in the centre of the board and surround it with the decorated utensils. Add information about the traditional designs to the silhouette.

Welsh Love Spoons

These are carved wooden spoons that were first made by young men in the 1600s as courtship gifts for their intended brides. Today they are still made and often given as presents for an anniversary, a wedding, a house warming etc. Love spoons are traditionally carved from one piece of wood. Each of the symbols chosen to decorate the handles have specific

meanings and thus convey a message e.g. horse shoe - good luck, wheel - I will work and provide for you, twist - togetherness, vines and leaves - love that will grow through the years, the bell and the cross - will you marry me, solid heart - full of love, harp - music of love, flower - love will blossom etc.

Equipment Needed

Plastic spoons, glue, squares of brown tissue paper (10 x 10 cm approx.), drawing pencils (4B-6B), scrap paper, scissors, pieces of brown sugar paper, black wax i.e. crayons, examples of Welsh Love Spoons.

Talk About

- The examples of Welsh Love Spoons, which part of the spoon is decorated and what each of the different symbols mean.
- Where else we see symbols that convey a message rather than words e.g. road signs, labels on clothes etc.
- Tearing tissue paper into small pieces and sticking it to cover the surface of a plastic spoon.
- Pressing the pieces down firmly so that the shape of the spoon remains apparent.
- How much glue to use and where to put it.
- Drawing round a spoon in pencil on scrap paper and then sketching symbols of their own design (or those from the actual spoons that they want to use) onto their spoon handle.
- Finding textured surfaces in the room and taking a rubbing from them.

Doing

- Ask the children to tear the tissue paper into small pieces and glue these pieces all over the spoon to cover it. (They may need to use further squares to complete the task). Tell them to give the finished spoon a final coat of glue all over to seal down the edges of the tissue paper.
- Ask the children to use black crayons and brown paper and to take rubbings of different textured surfaces in the room. These rubbings need to cover the paper.
- They now draw on the back of their paper of rubbings the symbols they are going to use to decorate their spoon. Finally cut them out.
- With the rubbing side upwards, they stick the symbols on to the handle of their spoon.

Display

Put a Welsh flag and information about Welsh Love Spoons in the middle of the board. Stick a loop of thread on to the back of each spoon handle and suspend them on individual pieces of coloured paper (green or red) in rows across the board. Ask the children to draw each of the symbols they have used plus their meaning in black pen on a strip of white paper and put these next to each spoon.

The Willow Pattern

Despite its appearance the willow pattern is not Chinese in origin. It was first designed by Thomas Minton about 1760 when there was a craze for collecting souvenirs from the east. In order to compete, English manufacturers copied and adapted many Chinese designs. At the Spode pottery works various motifs were combined into a blue and white pattern that was the first true Willow Pattern. The blue was a shade called cobalt blue. This pattern was copied and is still manufactured (sometimes in colours other than blue) and collected today around the world. The origin of the story is unknown, it was told in China more than a thousand years ago and brought to our country by the crusaders.

Equipment Needed

Blue paint and blue felt tip pens, pieces of card to use as palettes, thin strips of card and cotton buds for printing, small paper plates, pieces of scrap paper to practise on, coloured copies of the Willow Pattern design minus the border to fit in the centre of the plates, examples of the Willow Pattern design with a border as a stimulus and written versions of the Willow Pattern story.

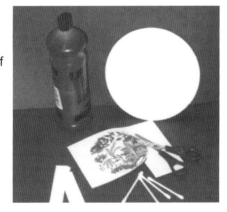

Talk About

- The Willow Pattern story asking the children to find the different characters and the different parts of the landscape as it is mentioned and to describe the colour cobalt blue.
- What a border pattern is and where it can be found on a Willow Pattern plate, plus some of the shapes found in the border pattern and how they are repeated in the design.
- Printing with pieces of thin card and cotton buds dipped in paint by pressing them on to paper and then lifting them off the paper- not smearing and spreading.
- Different ways of bending and using the pieces of card to create a variety of marks.

Doing

- Once the children have explored printing on paper and decided upon a design, give them a paper plate and discuss where they are going to add a printed pattern - around the edge as a border.
- Remind them that their pattern must to be a repeating one and that they will need to use each of the lines or dots they print in the same sequence, several times around the border.
- When the printed pattern is dry, further details could be added using the blue felt tip pens. This detail also needs repeating around the border. Finally stick the coloured copy of the willow pattern minus the border in the centre of each plate.

Display

Put a large cut out of a Willow Pattern plate in the centre of a board backed in blue, plus a printed out version (in blue) of the story. The patterned plates (each with a hanger, or loop of yarn on the back) could then be arranged in concentric circles around it.

Patterns from Europe

Ukrainian Easter Eggs

The custom of decorating eggs at Easter is popular throughout Europe. The egg is considered a symbol of fertility and rebirth and so, a symbol of spring. In the Ukraine, designs are drawn using wax and dye in a series of layers like batik. The wax is finally removed by holding the egg close to a candle flame to reveal the completed pattern. Ukrainian Easter eggs are usually decorated with geometric designs using colours and motifs that are symbolic and meaningful, e.g. white = innocence, yellow = the sun, orange = endurance/ warmth, green = nature / re-growth, red = the blood of Christ, black = maturity. The symbols include diamonds = knowledge, circles = completeness /continuity, ladders = prosperity, stars = love/caring, zig-zags = heat, straight lines = eternity, dots = stars or Mary's tears at the crucifixion, curls or spirals= protection etc.

Equipment Needed

Easter egg shapes cut out of white, black and coloured paper, strips (broad and narrow), triangles, diamonds and squares in varying sizes cut from coloured paper. Black felt tip pens, scissors, glue, cotton buds for printing, black, white and coloured paint, pieces of card as palettes, paint brushes and thin wax crayons plus examples of decorated Ukrainian Easter eggs from books and the Internet.

Talk About

- Where the Ukraine is on a map of Europe.
- What geometric means.
- The colours and shapes they can see on the pictures of the eggs and how they are arranged.
- What these colours and symbols mean and what we associate with them e.g. red for danger, a black cat for luck etc.
- The colours and cut out shapes they can choose, cut, alter and arrange to make a pattern on an egg shaped piece of paper.
- Printing with a cotton bud and a piece of card dipped in paint by pressing on and lifting off.
- Drawing patterns with thin wax crayons and then painting over the top of them and watching the wax resist the paint and keep the pattern.

Doing

- Once the children have an egg shaped piece of paper, scissors, strips and shapes of coloured paper, they need to alter and arrange these to make a geometric pattern on their egg shape. When they are happy with their design they glue it down. They outline some of the shapes using a black felt tip pen and add dots as further decoration with cotton buds dipped in black or white paint.
- Alternatively they could draw the patterns with wax crayons on white egg shaped paper before painting over them using a brush and coloured paint.

Display

Cut the silhouette of an Easter egg out of black paper for the centre of the board. Put the title of the display on this plus information about Ukrainian Easter eggs. Arrange the children's decorated eggs (individually mounted and cut round) around the silhouette. Leave a small space around each to emphasise its egg shape.

Polish Paper Cuts - Wycinanki

Wycinanki is a traditional Polish folk art. In past times country folk cut intricate mirror designs from paper, often using shears as their tool to do so. Roosters, flowers and geometric shapes were popular designs. These cut outs were used to decorate the beams and walls inside their houses particularly at Easter and Christmas when their homes were given a fresh coat of white paint. At this time the old Wycinanki were thrown out and new ones made. Wycinanki vary in different regions, in some they are of a single colour whereas in others they are multi-coloured.

Equipment Needed

Squares and circles of black sugar paper (20 x 20 cm approx.), brightly-coloured sticky-paper, scissors, glue and squares of white or grey paper to stick the cut outs on. Scrap paper, again in circles and squares, as practice paper for cut out designs, examples of Polish paper cuts and doilies.

Talk About

- Where Poland is and the examples of Polish paper-cuts. Ask them to describe how the papercuts were made and what they were used for.
- The different shapes used to make the patterns on the doilies and how these shapes are repeated in the design.
- Folding paper and cutting shapes from the folds to make a pattern, remembering to leave enough of the fold intact so that the shape doesn't fall to pieces.
- Refolding the same shape in other ways and cutting out further shapes to elaborate the pattern.
- Cutting small shapes from the coloured paper to decorate the cut shape.
- Arranging these shapes in a repetitive order rather than at random to keep a mirror image.
- Sticking these shapes down, how much glue to use and where to put it.

Doing

- Ask the children to choose a scrap paper circle or square and to explore folding it in different ways before cutting out a series of shapes along the folds. Then they can open the shape, refold it differently and make further cuts to create a pattern. They may need to repeat this several times before they are ready to do the same with a black sugar paper circle or square.
- They choose a variety of coloured sticky-paper squares to use for the decoration. In order to have a repetition of similar shapes, they must fold each square several time before cutting through the layers. The coloured shapes are then arranged on the black paper cut-out.
- Once they are happy with their arrangement and have checked that the shapes repeat in the same way on each part of the cut out they need to stick them down. Although they are using sticky paper it would be advisable to stick the shapes down with glue to make sure they are securely fixed.

Display

Arrange the completed designs individually mounted on squares of white paper, in equally spaced rows like a grid across the board. Make sure the gaps between each piece is fairly narrow for maximum impact.

Dutch Delft

Delft earthenware gets its name from the town of Delft in Holland where it was and still is made. This blue and white china was copied from Chinese porcelain brought to Holland in the 17th century by the Dutch East India Company. Delftware was originally made for everyday use and would have been found throughout the house as tiles, plates, jugs, vases, teapots etc. even as chamber pots, chandeliers and bird cages! Because such objects were prone to breakage relatively few of these household goods have survived. Delft china is still made and decorated as it was in the past with scenes showing windmills, sailing boats, the countryside and people dressed in traditional Dutch costume. It is world renowned and highly collectable.

Equipment Needed

Blue and white paint, pieces of card as palettes, paintbrushes, blue felt tip pens, drawing pencils (4B-6B), scrap paper, blue paper, squares of white paper or card (14 x 14 cm approx.) plus circles of white paper (10 or 11 cm in diameter) and blue circles slightly larger. Pictures of windmills, sailing boats, the countryside and examples of decorated Delft pottery plus travel brochures featuring Holland.

Talk About

- Where Holland is and where the town of Delft is.
- The colours and type of decoration on Delft china and tiles.
- Sketching a scene in pencil on scrap paper using the pictures, the travel brochures or the view from the window as a stimulus.
- Drawing this sketch inside a circle for use as a tile decoration and designing a motif to go in each corner of a tile.
- Mixing paint to make different shades of blue using one blue plus several tones created by the addition of various amounts of white.
- Drawing and outlining using a felt tip pen.

Doing

- Ask the children to make quick pencil sketches on scrap paper of scenes they might use on their tile plus a motif for the corners.
- They need to choose one sketch to use for their tile.
- They can mix a pale shade of blue paint on their palette and use it to draw the outline of their chosen shapes on a circle of white paper.

- Next they need to fill in the shapes with darker shades of blue using a brush and when the paint is dry to add details and further drawing e.g. leaves on trees, ripples on water etc. using either a brush or a blue felt tip pen.

- The completed circle needs to be stuck on to a blue circle of paper and then glued in the centre of a square of white paper. Finally a small motif needs to be cut and stuck in each corner of the square to complete the tile.

Display

Arrange the tiles in a circular arrangement on blue backing paper around the silhouette of a windmill and information about Holland and Delft pottery.

Spanish Ceramic Designs

The designs on Spanish ceramics show influences from other cultures, notably the Arabic style of the Moors who invaded the country, the European Renaissance and the neighbouring nearby Italy. Popular motifs include leaves, flowers, human figures and fantastic animals depicted in bright colours. The centres of large plates usually feature a spray of flowers surrounded by a concentric arrangement. In most towns and cities in Spain, decoratively tiled floors can be seen both inside and outside, as well as decorated pottery - mugs, plates, bowls etc. which are still used today.

Equipment Needed

Paper plates, squares of brightly coloured paper, coloured felt tip pens - broad and fine, glue and glue spreaders, flowers and leaves, pictures of flowers, drawing paper and pencils (4b-6b) and scrap paper for sketching plus examples of Spanish ceramic designs.

Talk About

- Where Spain is on the world map and the sort of objects that go under the heading of 'ceramics'.
- The decoration on plates and mugs etc. that they have at home.
- What a central motif is and what a border pattern is and where these would be found on a plate.
- Sketching the shapes of flowers and leaves in pencil on scrap paper before deciding on those to be used in a design.
- Cutting flower and leaf shapes out of coloured paper. Sticking these shapes on to a plate - how much glue to use and where to put it.
- Linking, decorating and adding to the shapes using felt tip pens.

Doing

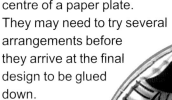

- Once the children have experimented with sketching leaves and flowers, they choose the shapes they want to use for the central design on their plate. Cut these shapes out of coloured paper and arrange them in the centre of a paper plate. They may need to try several arrangements before they arrive at the final design to be glued down.

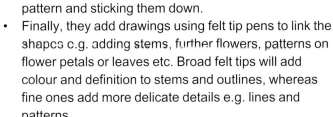
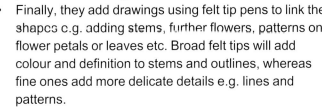

- Next they decide on the leaf/ flower shapes they are going to use as a border pattern around the edge of the plate. They need to cut several versions of each shape before arranging them in a repeating pattern and sticking them down.

- Finally, they add drawings using felt tip pens to link the shapes e.g. adding stems, further flowers, patterns on flower petals or leaves etc. Broad felt tips will add colour and definition to stems and outlines, whereas fine ones add more delicate details e.g. lines and patterns.

Display

Attach calendar hangers or loops of string with sellotape to the back of each plate. Put examples of Spanish ceramic designs and information about them in the centre of the board surrounded by a concentric arrangement of plates.

Patterns from Europe

The Greek Key Patterns

There are several versions of this pattern from the ancient world and it is often found as a border on textiles and ceramics. Drawn as a continuous running pattern it is said to symbolise the everlasting circle of life. As a broken swastika style pattern this maze like design represented good luck and well being to the ancient Greeks.

Equipment Needed

Dot lattice maths paper cut into strips 10 cm wide approx. glue, pencils, rulers, felt tip pens in brown, red, yellow, black and orange. Pictures of Greek vases or fabric that show the pattern.

Talk About

- Identify Greece on a map of Europe.
- Where the Greek Key Pattern can be seen and what it looks like.
- How the same shapes are continuously repeated in a row to make up the pattern and how the shapes are joined together.
- What a border pattern is and where it is likely to be found on fabric, pottery etc.
- Joining the dots on the dot lattice grid together to form shapes similar to those in the Greek Key Pattern using a ruler to keep the lines straight.
- Drawing a series of similar shapes in a row to make a repeating pattern.
- Combining lines of colour in different ways using felt tip pens.

Doing

- Ask the children to choose a strip of dot lattice paper and to sketch out in pencil their design for a Greek Key Pattern.

- Remind them to keep repeating the same shape / shapes throughout their pattern and to make sure the shapes are joined up at the base.
- When they are happy with their design they draw over the pencil lines with a black felt tip pen, using a ruler to keep the lines straight.
- Using different coloured felt tip pens, they now need to decorate, outline and fill parts of their pattern using lines.
- Remind them to use the same colours in the same way as they decorate each of the shapes in their pattern, to keep the pattern a repeating one.
- Each child could produce several versions of the Greek Key pattern.

Display

Use these strips as a border around the edge of a board that has information and pictures about the ancient Greeks. Or arrange them, unmounted, as a block, each one touching its neighbour, with a thin black border. Surround the block with black silhouettes of different shaped Greek vases, urns etc.

Russian Nesting Dolls - Matryoshka

Matryoshka are brightly painted wooden dolls made to be taken apart to reveal smaller dolls fitting inside one another. The name is derived from the Latin word for mother and is seen as the symbol of motherhood and fertility, by depicting the image of a mother of a big family who is very healthy and has a portly figure. The most traditional design is one that shows a young Russian woman in native costume with a scarf on her head and wearing an apron decorated with flowers, usually in red, yellow or blue. In the past female artists painted the clothes and male artists painted the faces. Nowadays they are completed by either. In traditional sets all of the dolls look almost identical to one another, and the number of dolls in a set ranges from 5 to 30.

Equipment Needed

Squares of white paper (approx. 3 or 4 per child) that vary in length, drawing pencils (4B-6B) coloured felt tip pens, pink paper for the dolls' faces, white doilies, brightly coloured paper, glue and scissors plus pictures or models of Russian Nesting Dolls.

Talk About

- The different sizes, but similar shapes of the dolls in each group; the sort of clothes they are wearing and how each doll has matching features and clothes on a smaller or larger scale.
- The number of doll shapes (3 or 4) they need to draw and how each shape needs to be a different size on a different sized piece of paper.
- Which pieces of paper will be best for the largest shape and which for the smallest.
- Drawing features with felt tip pens, and cutting flower shapes and leaves from coloured paper for decoration,

remembering that each doll will need to match the other members of its group.

Doing

- Ask the children to choose a piece of paper for their largest doll shape and to sketch its outline before cutting it out.
- Now ask them to draw and cut out a matching shape on a smaller piece of paper. They continue in the same way on other smaller pieces until they have several similar shapes that decrease in size. Leave the choice of how many shapes to each child.
- Stick circles of pink for the faces on to the heads of the doll shapes and draw in their features in black felt tip pen.
- Colour around the faces as though they are wearing scarves and draw in the part where the scarf ties under the chin.
- The bottom of each shape needs a band of colour before a doily is stuck above it as the bottom of the apron.
- Add cut out flowers and leaves as decoration on the rest of the body.

Display

Place information about Russian dolls and a map of Russia in the middle of the board and arrange each group of dolls as a family in rows from the largest to the smallest around it.

Braiding from Lapland

The Lapps or Sami as they prefer to be called are nomadic people who herd reindeer in the northern parts of Scandinavia (Sweden, Norway and Finland) near or above the Arctic circle. The technique for woven and braided bands is known throughout the Nordic countries but what is special about Sami woven bands are the specific colours and patterns - red, yellow, green and blue - that denote the district of their homeland. The North Sami bands are the most colourful with flower motives and geometric patterns whereas those in the central and southern areas have less decoration and chequered patterns are typical. These woven bands are used as decoration on the hem of the kolt or tunic which is the traditional dress, on hats, as a belt or sash or for bags, shoe bands etc.

Equipment Needed

Travel brochures showing Lapps wearing their traditional costume in their natural setting. Glue, scissors, pencils, rulers and sellotape. Strips of red, yellow, green and blue paper 7cm x 30cm plus narrow strips 1cm wide in the same colours.

Talk About

- The part of the world in which the Lapps live and where it is found on a map of the world. What a braid is and what we use braids for e.g. to tie hair, to decorate clothes, cushions or textiles and when we wrap presents.
- Making a paper loom from a strip of paper - where and how to measure using a pencil and ruler (top to bottom with 1 cm between each line) and where to cut (along the lines stopping 2cm from the top each time - see illustration.)

- Weaving with the narrow strips over and under the cut strips of the loom - remembering to alternate the start of each row e.g. if the first row starts by weaving over the first strip then the second row will start under it.
- Placing and arranging the narrow strips in rows to make a pattern before starting to weave. Remind them that their pattern needs to be a repeating one i.e. the colours need to be arranged in the same sequence throughout.
- Pushing the woven strips closely together and fastening each completed row to the loom on the back using sellotape.

Doing

- Once the children have chosen and converted their widest strips of paper into looms they need to choose narrower strips to weave with.
- Remind them to repeat the same sequence of colours throughout their weaving e.g. 3 green strips followed by 1 red one, again followed by 3 green strips and 1 red one.
- Tell them to bend the ends of each of their woven strips over the back of the loom and stick them down using sellotape to keep them in place.

Display

Arrange the information, pictures and a map in the centre of the board and use the unmounted woven strips to create rows around it, each strip touching its neighbour. Leave a small gap between each row.

Adinkra Printed Cloth

Adinkra is a traditional dyed Ghanaian cloth on which black symbols are printed using calabash shell printing blocks. Lines are drawn on to the cloth with a large comb dipped in dye to create rectangular boxes in which the symbols are printed. Each symbol, of which there are over fifty, has a special meaning. Dark brown or red Adinkra cloth is traditionally worn at funerals whereas bright colours are more usual on festive occasions.

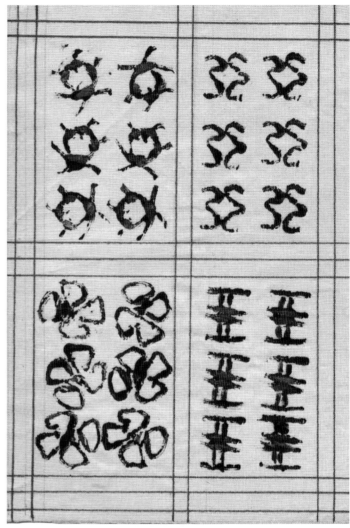

Equipment Needed

Plasticine, clay or other mouldable material to make printing blocks from (Wax Works was used here). Black fabric felt tip pens, glue, rulers, food colouring, black paint, paint brushes, pieces of sponge and pieces of white cotton fabric plus examples of Adinkra Textiles from the Internet.

Talk About

- Where Ghana is on a map of Africa.
- The patterns on the Adinkra cloth and how they are set out.
- Each symbol having a specific meaning and where we see symbols e.g. on clothes and what they mean.
- Making shapes out of mouldable material by rolling and pressing it and inventing their own symbol shapes and recording what they mean.
- Sticking these shapes to card with glue to make printing blocks.
- Putting paint on them with a brush before pressing them on to the fabric and lifting them off to reveal the shapes they have printed.
- Colouring fabric with sponge dipped in diluted food colouring.

Doing

- The children first colour their fabric with food colouring and leave it to dry whilst they make the shapes for their printing blocks. They then need to use a ruler and a black felt tip pen to rule lines horizontally and vertically quite close together to outline a series of large rectangles on the fabric.
- Next they choose a printing block, put black paint on it with a brush and press it on to the fabric several times inside one of the rectangles. They then need to choose a second shape to print inside a different rectangle. Continue until all the rectangles have been filled.

Display

Mount the work individually on black. Ask the children to draw their shapes and give their meaning. Mount these also on black. Back the board in blue and arrange the mounted fabric in rows and add the drawn symbols and explanations underneath each one.

Zulu Bead Patterns

Glass beads from foreign traders found their way to South Africa in the 19th century when they became popular as decorations on ceremonial dress. Prior to this, shells, teeth, wood and clay were used. Originally only those honoured by the king were allowed imported beads. Owning large quantities of beads and beadwork was a statement of power and influence and today beaded finery is still used to indicate differences in marital status, gender, age and occupation. Geometrical motifs and interlacing patterns in red, blue, yellow, green, orange, white and black are the most popular.

Equipment Needed

Squares of black sugar paper 15 x 15 cm, scissors, glue. Red, yellow, green, blue and orange paper cut into strips of different widths x 15 cm, cotton buds, white paint, pieces of card as palettes plus examples of Zulu Bead patterns from travel brochures and the Internet.

Talk About

*   Where South Africa is on a map of the African Continent.
*   What geometric means and the names of some geometric shapes and where they can be seen in the Zulu bead patterns.
*   Folding a strip of coloured paper in half lengthwise and then in half again before cutting a zig zag into the top and bottom of the folded strip and removing the pieces. Then cutting a zig zag into the sides of the strip remembering to leave a hinge above and below it before opening the cut strip to reveal a repeating pattern. Folding further strips and cutting different shapes from them.
*   Printing dots with a cotton bud dipped in paint.

Doing

*   Once the children have cut patterns in several coloured strips they need to arrange them in rows across a piece of black paper with a gap between each row. When they are happy with their arrangement it needs to be stuck it down. Some of the shapes cut out whilst making the patterns could be added to the design.
*   To add a 'bead' effect, the children use a cotton bud dipped in white paint to print rows of white dots on, inside, above and below the cut patterns.

Display

The unmounted work could de displayed as a block, each piece touching its neighbour, with a wide border around the edge and information added below.

19

Adire Cloth Patterns

The patterns on Adire cloth from Nigeria are made by drawing or stencilling on the fabric with a wax like paste made from cassava flour using chicken feathers. The cloth is then dipped in indigo dye. The drawn patterns resist the dye and remain white whilst the rest of the fabric turns deep blue. The symbols drawn on the fabric are usually repeated within a grid and often tell a story or have a meaning or message about the person or society which created the cloth.

Equipment Needed

Thin white wax crayons, white cotton fabric, masking tape, paintbrushes, newspaper, rulers, blue and black food colouring. Examples of Adire cloth patterns from the Internet.

Talk About

- Where Nigeria is on a map of Africa.
- The shapes in the patterns on the Adire cloth. What they might represent or mean and where they are repeated.
- Drawing new shapes of their own and giving them a meaning.
- What colour indigo is. Mixing blue and a little black food colouring together to make a darker shade of blue.

- Sticking fabric on to the work surface with strips of masking tape to stop it from moving about before drawing on it with a thin white wax crayon.
- What a grid is and how to draw a grid using a ruler.

Doing

- Once the children have taped their fabric to the work surface they need to draw lines on it using a ruler and a thin white wax crayon, to divide it into a series of rectangles.
- Inside each rectangle they need to draw one of their symbols, again in white wax crayon - the **same** symbol can be repeated more than once.
- Now remove the tape, place the fabric on newspaper and having mixed blue and '**very little**' black food colouring together to make dark blue. Use a brush to paint this all over the fabric to reveal the patterns that have been drawn.

Display

Mount the pieces of work individually with their drawn symbols as a key under each one. Display them in rows, each piece close to its neighbour, around a map of Africa and information about Adire cloth. Add photographs and writing about how the children made their own version of it.

Kente Cloth Patterns

Kente cloth of the Ashanti people of Africa represents their values, history and beliefs. Woven in narrow strips that are then sewn together, Kente cloth was originally reserved for royalty and its use limited to special occasions. Nowadays it is available to anyone who can afford it and although it is often machine printed it is still regarded as a symbol of nobility and social standing. Patterns and motifs are generally created by the weaver and are usually geometric representations of objects with a specific meaning. There are over 300 types of cloth designs. Colours also have specific meanings e.g. Yellow - royalty, wealth and vitality, Pink - calmness and tenderness, Red - sacrifice and struggle, Blue - good fortune and harmony, Green - growth and prosperity, Purple - healing, Black - links with ancestral spirits.

Equipment Needed

Pieces of coloured paper A4 size, brown or black pieces of A4 paper as a background, glue and examples of Kente cloth patterns from books and the Internet.

Talk About

- Where the cloth originates using a map of Africa.
- The patterns on the Kente cloth, how the colours and shapes are arranged and how they are repeated on alternate or adjacent rows.
- Tearing pieces of paper into long strips and short strips, thick strips and thin strips - old faded backing paper is ideal for practice pieces.
- Arranging the same colours and lengths in rows to make a repeating pattern.
- Arranging some of the strips horizontally and some vertically in the pattern.
- Sticking the strips down - how much glue to use and where to put it.

Doing

- Tell the children to choose the colours for their pattern - suggest they limit it to four or five to make it easier to repeat them in their design.
- They need to decide which colours are going to be torn into long strips and arranged in rows vertically and which ones are going to be torn into short strips and arranged horizontally. Also which strips are going to be thick and which are going to be thin.
- When they have torn several strips, suggest they arrange and stick these down on a piece of background paper as the first row of their pattern.

- They then arrange a second row in a different way and stick these pieces down next to the first row.
- They continue and complete their pattern, copying the shapes and colours from each row in the same order until the background paper is covered.

Display

Arrange the unmounted work as a block in the middle of the board surrounded with a border. Add the words 'Kente Cloth Patterns' several times on the border around the block. Display information about the patterns under the board.

Ndebele Houses

The Ndebele people of South Africa are renowned for mural painting on the walls of their homes. Painting is done exclusively by women, young girls being taught by their mothers. A well painted home - usually a mud walled house - shows that a woman is a good wife and mother. She is responsible for the painting of the outside gates, front walls, side walls and usually the interior of the home. First the walls are whitewashed. They are then decorated with geometric patterns and shapes with black outlines which are later filled in with colour. Originally paints were natural coloured clays. Five main colours are used, red, yellow, sky blue, green and sometimes pink. The meaning of these colours is symbolic e.g. they can mean status or power, offer prayers, announce a marriage etc.

Equipment Needed

Drawing pencils (4B-6B), rulers, black felt tip pens, white paper 24 x 20 cm approx., brown paper, scissors, glue and pieces of brightly coloured paper (red, blue, green, yellow and pink). Examples of geometric shapes and Ndebele decorated houses from books and the Internet.

Talk About

*   Where South Africa is on a map of the African Continent.
*   The names of the geometric shapes decorating the Ndebele houses, where similar shapes can be seen and how they are arranged.
*   Drawing similar shapes in pencil on folded pieces of coloured paper and cutting them out so that shapes will match and be similar in size.
*   Drawing rectangles of different sizes using a pencil and a ruler
*   Gluing the shapes down to make a pattern and outlining them using a thick black felt tip pen and a ruler.

Doing

*   Children place paper landscape way up and draw a line in pencil across their paper. This is where the roof will finally be glued to the house.
*   Below this line the children draw a door and windows on their paper and colour these shapes in black. Then they draw rectangular shapes between, above and below the windows and door first in pencil and then black felt tip pen. They cut shapes from the coloured paper and arrange them to make patterns inside the rectangles and stick them down.

*   Next they outline and draw inside some of the shapes to add further decoration using a black felt tip pen and a ruler if necessary.
*   Finally they get a piece of brown paper, cut it into a roof shape for their Ndebele house and stick it along the line at the top of the paper.

Display

Put a large black silhouette of a Ndebele house in the middle of the board and arrange the children's Ndebele houses in rows around it. Add information and pictures about Ndebele houses to the silhouette. Put a map and books about Africa under or next to the display.

Bogolan Mud Cloth - Bogolanfini

This cloth, with its stark black, white and brown patterns, originates with the Bamama people who live in Mali. White cloth, usually woven by men, is first washed and then dipped in a brown solution made from leaves. As it dries it takes on a yellow colour and is ready to be drawn on. It is decorated with mud, usually by women, using small pieces of bamboo and flat metal. The mud is collected from ponds and left to ferment in a pot for a year during which time it becomes black. The cloth is then washed to remove the mud and the whole process repeated again. Finally caustic soda is used to bleach parts of the pattern white. The symbols and colours used refer to Bamama history and mythology. Black and white are traditional colours for story telling. Rust is popular as it is supposed to have supernatural powers to protect hunters, and white is worn by girls and women in ceremonial events.

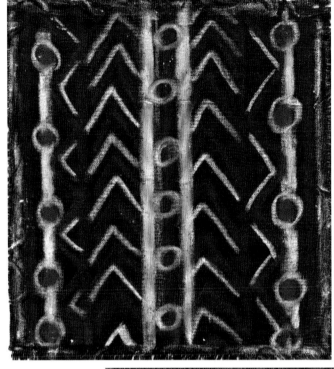

Equipment Needed

Pieces of white cotton fabric, black, white and brown oil pastel crayons, paintbrushes, newspaper, masking tape, black food colouring and cold black coffee or cold wet used tea bags, books and pictures from the Internet showing mud cloth patterns.

Talk About

- Finding Mali on a map of Africa.
- The colours and shapes on the cloth and how they make up patterns.
- Drawing similar shapes on fabric with oil pastels.
- Taping the fabric to the work surface first so that it doesn't move.
- Painting with food colouring, or a teabag, to colour the fabric.

Doing

- Once the children have taped their fabric to the work surface, they can draw a pattern on it using black, white and brown oil pastels.

They can draw symbols that are similar to those found on the mud cloth in the pictures. Remind them to press on firmly so that the marks they draw are fairly thick.

- They now remove the tape, place the fabric on a piece of newspaper and paint all over the fabric with food colouring or a teabag. Their patterns should now be in evidence on a brown or black background.

Display

Arrange the unmounted pieces of work as a block in the middle of the board surrounded by a border of black and then a second border of brown. Add a title to the border and display pictures and information about mud cloth under or next to the board.

Maasai Jewellery

The Maasai are a Kenyan tribe that constantly move with their cattle. Their beadwork jewellery indicates where they come from and their status. The women of the tribe shave their heads and wear banded necklaces and earrings made up of thousands of glass and plastic beads on special occasions. Men wear beaded arm and leg bands made for them as a sign of love. Jewellery is always made by women and the colours used - red, white, green, blue, orange, yellow and black follow the strict rules of the tribe. Symmetry in a design is avoided. Colours shapes and patterns all have a meaning e.g. red is the tribal colour, blue is the sky and the gods, and green is the fresh grassland. Women amass necklaces throughout their lives which reveal their status, age group, whether they are married and even whether they have given birth to a son.

Equipment Needed

White ready mix paint, cotton buds, pieces of card as palettes, circles cut from grey sugar paper and red, orange, green, yellow and blue paper (16 cm diameter), blue paper A4 size, pencils, black felt tip pens, scissors and glue. Books showing pictures of Maasai jewellery e.g. travel brochures, plus examples from the Internet.

Talk About

*   Where Kenya is on a map of Africa.
*   The size, colours and patterns on the Maasai beaded necklaces and what it might be like to wear one.
*   Folding a circular shape in half and cutting along the fold to make a semi-circle.
*   Cutting curved strips from a semi-circle.
*   Drawing and cutting a head and neck shape from brown paper.
*   Printing with cotton buds by dipping them into paint.

Doing

*   Tell the children to fold a grey sugar paper circle in half and cut along the fold. Tell them to keep one of the semi-circles to work on.

*   Using the coloured paper, again folded and cut into semi-circles, the children need to cut curved strips from the different colours following the curved part of the shape. They can then arrange and glue these in rows across the grey sugar paper semi-circle. They can add straight strips of coloured paper to section the collar.
*   A head and neck need to be drawn and cut from brown paper, then stuck on blue A4 paper. Then the decorated semi-circle needs to be stuck below the head and neck to form a collar.
*   Further decoration to the collar needs to be added by printing, using a cotton bud dipped in white paint.
*   Finally the children need to draw features on the face using a felt tip.
*   Add a head band and narrow strips of paper as earrings. Cut round the completed work leaving a narrow band of blue and add narrow strips of paper as earrings.

Display

Arrange information about Maasai jewellery in the middle of the board with the individual heads and their beaded collars in rows around it.

Ancient Egyptian Patterns

The Ancient Egyptians painted decorative patterns as well as hieroglyphs (picture symbols) on the ceilings and walls of their tombs. These patterns repeated chosen colours and shapes as a grid and were similar to the patterns of the woven matting originally used to line the tombs. Popular colours were blue, red, yellow, green, black and white which were alternated throughout the design. Motifs included spirals, lotus and lily flowers and geometric shapes.

Equipment Needed

Pieces of white paper A4 size, strips of coloured paper (6cm wide approx.) in Egyptian colours, rulers, pencils, scissors, glue and examples of Egyptian motifs from books and the Internet.

Talk About

- Egypt and where it is found on a map of Africa.
- The different motifs and colours found in the patterns.
- What a repeat pattern is and what a grid is.
- Folding the strips of paper over before cutting shapes out of them so that the outcome is several matching shapes.
- Arranging the shapes to form a pattern on the grid - on top of, between, next to and joining each other.
- Using the tile facility on a computer graphics programme to draw motifs similar to those on the right, to produce similar patterns.

Doing

- First the children cut equal sized squares in two colours and arrange them as a repeat pattern on a piece of white paper. Next stick them down.

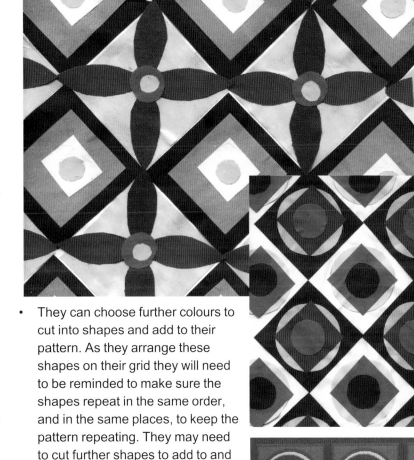

- They can choose further colours to cut into shapes and add to their pattern. As they arrange these shapes on their grid they will need to be reminded to make sure the shapes repeat in the same order, and in the same places, to keep the pattern repeating. They may need to cut further shapes to add to and build up their pattern.
- Similar designs to those illustrated could be drawn using a computer graphics package (Dazzle has been used here) and then tiled for an all over pattern.

Display

Cut a black silhouette of pyramids to go in the centre of the board with the title. Individually mount the work and arrange it in rows around the title. Keep the spaces between the pieces work and between the rows equal.

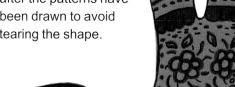

Patterns from India

Mehndi Patterns

These patterns are painted on the palms of women's hands and often feature flowers or geometric designs. In the case of a bride the name or initials of her husband to be are included. The bride will also have the back of her hands and her feet decorated. Mehndi designs are symbols of good fortune and prosperity and are usually associated with festive occasions. The patterns are drawn using henna powder mixed with water and made into a paste. Henna is made from the dried leaves of the myrtle shrub. Traditionally bands of patterns are drawn on the fingers with a different pattern on the palm and the finger tips are painted with solid colour. When the dried paste has been removed the designs remain, orange / brown in colour, and will stay on the skin for a few days especially if they are rubbed over with lemon juice.

Equipment Needed

Pieces of skin coloured paper (beige, peach, pink etc.) pencils, scissors and fine brown felt tipped pens, pictures of Mehndi patterns from books and the Internet.

Talk About

- Where India is on a world map.
- The shapes and designs seen in the pictures of Mehndi patterns.
- Festive occasions for which we dress up to celebrate.
- What colour henna is.
- The names of the different parts of the hand - including the palm.
- Drawing round a hand with a pencil - either their own hand or their neighbour's hand. The hand to be drawn around needs to be kept as still as possible and the fingers arranged slightly apart.
- Using scissors to cut round the drawn shape carefully.
- Drawing patterns with a felt tip pen and where to draw them on a hand shape.

Doing

- Ask the children to choose a piece of coloured paper and to draw round their hand or their neighbour's hand.
- Tell them to choose a brown felt tip pen and to colour in the tips of each of the fingers on the shape they have drawn.
- They now need to draw rows of matching patterns on the rest of each finger before adding a further pattern to fill or cover the remaining part of the hand shape.
- Finally using scissors they carefully cut out their decorated hand shape - this is done after the patterns have been drawn to avoid tearing the shape.

Display

Mount each of the decorated hands on brown paper. Cut round each shape leaving a margin of brown paper around each one. Put the title 'Mehndi Patterns' in the middle of the board and arrange the hands in circular bands around it - palms pointing inwards, fingers pointing outwards.

Rangoli Patterns

These are floor patterns made to decorate Hindu homes in the State of Gujerat at festival times, especially during Diwali. They are based on a grid which is made using either pinches of powdered colour made from dried flowers, leaves, spices, burnt earth or charcoal or dots of coloured chalk. The patterns which are usually symmetrical and either square or circular round a central motif are then drawn on the grid and filled in with powdered colour. Traditional motifs with special significance are the lotus flower (creation and purity) the swastika (the changing world turning around an unchanging centre - God) and the figure 4 shown by the use of squares, four flowers with four petals and the swastika displaying four branches.

Equipment Needed

Dot lattice maths paper cut into squares, 21 x 21 cm approx., drawing pencils (4b-6b), rulers, black felt tip pens, coloured chalks and pictures of Rangoli patterns in books and from the Internet.

Talk About

- Where India and Bengal are on a map of the world.
- What symmetry means and what a grid is.
- The shapes found in the patterns - which part is the border and which is the central motif in the patterns.
- Drawing a symmetrical pattern on a grid by joining up the dots to make shapes using a pencil and a ruler.
- Drawing on top of the pencil lines with a black felt tip pen and a ruler, turning the paper to avoid smudging.
- Filling in shapes using chalks, pressing on firmly for a rich covering of colour and taking care not to colour or smudge outside the shapes.

Doing

- Tell the children to choose paper with a dot lattice grid on it, a pencil and a ruler and to lightly begin to sketch out the design of their pattern. If they only draw feint lines they will be able to rub them out easily if they want to alter their pattern.
- Remind them that the shapes on opposite sides of the pattern need to match and that there needs to be a different shape on its own in the centre.
- Once the pattern has been sketched they need to draw on top of the pencil lines using a ruler and a black felt tip pen.
- They fill in the shapes in their pattern using chalks taking care not to go outside the black lines. Remind

them that matching shapes need to be filled in with matching colours to keep the pattern symmetrical.
- Spray the finished patterns with hair spray to fix the chalk in place.

Display

Cover the board with black paper and individually mount the patterns on black first and then white. Mark out a dot lattice grid in white chalk in the centre of the board and display the title on this. Surround the grid with the patterns arranged in rows with small equal spaces between each pattern and each row.

Alpana Patterns

These floor patterns, similar to Rangoli patterns, are made to decorate the entrance to homes in the state of Bengal on special occasions such as births, weddings and festivals. The patterns are drawn on the ground with a cloth, or fingers soaked in rice paste, and are made up of lines and loops. Each pattern must be made up of unbroken lines drawn in a clockwise direction with no gaps for evil spirits to enter. Similar patterns called Kolam patterns are to be found in other parts of India.

Equipment Needed

Squares of brown paper (20 x 20cm approx.), pencils, white paint, fine paint brushes, pieces of card to use as palettes, white oil pastel crayons and examples of Alpana patterns from books and the Internet.

Talk About

- Where India and Bengal are on a map of the world.
- The arrangement of shapes within the patterns.
- Following the lines with their fingers to see if they are unbroken and that the shapes are linked together.
- What clockwise means.
- Drawing unbroken lines, loops and shapes on the work top with a finger making sure it moves in a clockwise direction.
- Finding the centre of the paper using a ruler in order to work the design around it.
- Drawing lines, loops and shapes with a paintbrush making sure that the paint used is always thick.
- Drawing lines, loops and shapes with an oil pastel crayon by pressing on firmly to make strong definite marks.

Doing

- Give the children a piece of brown paper. Help them find and mark the middle of it using a ruler and mark it faintly with a pencil dot.
- Suggest the children sketch out a circular pattern of shapes, loops and lines lightly round this central mark. Remind them that all the lines, loops and shapes must be joined together and that they should work in a clockwise direction - allow for some cheating here !
- When their pencil patterns are complete they work either with a thin brush and white paint or a white oil pastel - or a combination of both - and draw carefully on top of their pencil lines.

- The paint must be thick so that the lines are bold and the oil pastels need to be used firmly to have a similar effect.
- Encourage the children to start working on the centre of their pattern first and to turn their paper as they work to avoid smudging.

Display

Double mount the patterns individually, first on black and then white. Back the board with brown paper and put the title, 'Examples of Alpana Patterns', information etc. in the middle of the board. Arrange the individually mounted patterns in rows around this. Leave small equal spaces between each piece and between each row.

Appliqué Designs

Appliqué is a decorative design made by sewing pieces of material cut into different sizes and shapes on to a plain background, similar to patchwork. It is traditional in the State of Gujerat.

Popular motifs cut from bold colours include elephants, parrots, peacocks, flowers, plants and geometric shapes arranged as a sunburst or a square. The finished designs are made into bed coverings, door canopies and wall hangings. Wall hangings are known as chakla.

Equipment Needed

Squares of white paper (21x 21 cm approx.), scissors, glue, pieces of black paper and coloured paper, coloured felt tip pens, polar graph maths paper, and pictures of Indian appliqué designs from books and the Internet.

Talk About

- Where India and the state of Gujerat are on a map of the world.
- What appliqué means and how it is done.
- Which of the patterns are sunburst patterns and which are squares.
- The colours and shapes used in the patterns and the borders.
- Using polar graph paper to start off a sunburst pattern and colouring it in using felt tip pens.
- Cutting coloured paper into squares, triangles and circles and cutting animal, bird or flower shapes, out of black or coloured paper.
- Arranging and sticking cut shapes to make a pattern on white paper.
- How much glue to use and where to put it.

Doing

- Ask the children to choose which sort of pattern they want to make - squares or sunburst.
- If they choose to make a sunburst pattern they need a piece of polar graph paper and coloured felt tip pens. They fill in the shapes working from the centre outwards - suggest they limit the colours to 3 or 4 as this will make it easier for them to create a pattern. They will need to reduce the polar graph paper in size before they start so that a complete circle will fit in the middle of the white background paper.

- Once it is coloured and stuck down they cut shapes from the black or coloured paper to add to and extend the pattern further. Some areas could also be decorated with drawn and filled shapes using the felt tips.
- If they choose to make a square pattern they need to cut some squares from coloured paper and arrange them as a group in rows that touch each other on a piece of white paper, leaving space around the edge of the group for a border.
- Once the squares have been stuck down they cut smaller different shapes e.g. flowers, birds etc. to stick on top of the squares.
- Finally they cut a series of small identical shapes to arrange and stick as a border around the edge of the design remembering to leave a gap between it and the central pattern.

Display

Double mount the completed pieces of work individually, first on black and then on red, and arrange them in equally spaced rows around a title.

Patterns from India

Block Printing

Blocks of wood have designs cut into them using a file or hand drill. These are then dipped into dye and pressed on to plain fabric to print a pattern. For an all over repeating pattern each print needs to be made in line with the previous one. Sometimes pattern is made up with a central motif and a border. A long block with several repeating motifs is cut and used for the border and a larger single motif used for the main design.

Equipment Needed

Squares and strips of press print, coloured paper A4 size and squares 20x 20 cm approx., biros, scissors, water based printing ink, rollers and inking trays, examples of Indian block printed textiles from books and the Internet.

Talk About

- The colours and shapes in the patterns. Which patterns are repeat patterns and which patterns have a central motif and a border.
- Drawing lines and shapes into press print using a biro, pressing down firmly to ensure the design will print when it is inked up.
- Cutting shapes out of press print.
- Putting ink on an inking tray and rolling a roller across it to cover the roller with ink before running the inky roller across the surface of press print and placing the inked side on to paper, pressing down firmly for an even print.
- The shapes and sizes of press print needed for a central motif, a border pattern and a repeat pattern. Make sure the children try them for size on the pieces of coloured paper before they draw on them and ink them up.

Doing

- Once the children have decided on the sort of pattern they want to print, they choose the appropriate sizes of press print and cut it down if necessary, before drawing

shapes into it using a biro.
- They now choose the colour of paper they want to print on, ink up their pieces of press print using a roller and press it on to their paper.

- If they are going to print a central motif and a border the central motif needs to be printed first. Remind the children to turn their paper as they print the border along each edge to avoid smudging.
- If they are going to print a repeat pattern they need to make sure each time they use their inked up design that it is close to and touching the previous print. They need to re-ink their press print several times as they work to avoid the pattern becoming feint.
- If the designs the children have drawn fail to show up when printed, tell them to wipe their tiles clean and go over their drawing again, pressing in more firmly and then to ink them up and print once more.

Display

Mount the pieces of work individually and display them in two groups, one for the repeat patterns and one for the patterns with borders. Arrange the pieces in each group in rows with small spaces between them and between the rows.

Shisha Embroidery - Mirror Work

In many parts of India, cushions, bags and clothing are covered with mirror (shisha work) - the word shisha means little glass in Hindi and traditional mirrors are made from blown glass which is silvered on the back. In shisha work small circular mirrors are attached to the cloth with buttonhole stitch and lines of chain stitch mark out the pattern surrounding them. Shapes in the pattern such as diamonds, triangles and flower shapes are filled in with satin stitch. Shisha work is linked to three Islamic beliefs, one that mirrors will trap the evil eye and hold its reflection for eternity, two that mirrors will ward off the evil eye by reflecting it away from the wearer and three that mirrors will dazzle the evil eye so that it will go blind or blink and miss you.

Equipment Needed

Strips and squares of silver foil, black felt tip pens, squares of red, yellow and pink paper (20 x 20 cm approx.), glue, scissors, pictures of shisha work from books and from the Internet, and books showing different embroidery stitches.

Talk About

- Where India is on a map of the world.
- The shape and colours found in the patterns and how and where the mirrors are arranged and what size they are.
- What buttonhole stitch, chain stitch and satin stitch look like.

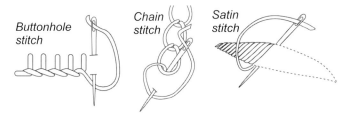

Buttonhole stitch *Chain stitch* *Satin stitch*

- Drawing loops and short lines with felt tip pens.
- Cutting small equally sized circles from foil by folding it over several times before the shapes are cut.
- Arranging circles of foil in a pattern on a piece of background paper leaving plenty of space between each one.

Doing

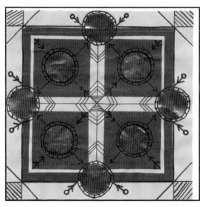

- The children first fold the foil and cut out their small circular mirror shapes. They choose a background paper and arrange the shapes in a pattern in the middle of the square, leaving room for a border around the edge.
- Once they are happy with their pattern and have made sure there is space for drawing around each circle, they stick it down.
- Using a black felt tip pen, they draw around each foil circle with small loops. Other shapes, using loops and lines, are drawn around and between the circles to join them together.
- Some of these shapes could then be filled in with short lines close together like satin stitch.
- The completed pattern finally needs a border of shapes and strips cut from paper decorated using a felt tip pen.

Display

Either arrange the work in colour groups i.e. all the patterns on red paper together, each piece touching its neighbour or individually mount each piece of work on black and arrange them in rows as a border around information about shisha work.

Patterns from the Middle and Far East

Mandala Designs

Mandalas are usually made from paper, textiles or coloured sand. They are pictorial symbols of the universe for Hindus and Buddhists (especially in India, Tibet, Nepal, China and Japan) who use them to help them to meditate. The word Mandala means circle and represents wholeness and the movement of energy from a central point. Mandala designs are symmetrical and are made up of circles, squares, rectangles, triangles, pentagons and other geometric shapes inside either a circle, square or rectangle.

Equipment Needed

Pre-cut circles of white paper approx. 20 cm in diameter, rulers, pencils, thin wax crayons, geometric shapes to draw round, scrap paper, black felt-tip pens and pictures of Mandalas from books and the Internet.

Talk About

- Where India, Tibet, Nepal, China and Japan are on a map of the world.
- What Hindus are and what Buddhists are.
- What meditate means and what helps them to concentrate or think.
- The names of the geometric shapes and different ways of arranging them inside a circle.
- What symmetrical means.
- Drawing round shapes with a pencil and using a ruler to draw geometric shapes of their own.
- Drawing lines using a felt tip pen and a ruler.
- Sketching several designs in pencil on scrap paper.
- Filling in shapes using wax crayons, pressing on firmly for a rich covering of colour.

Doing

- Allow the children to sketch various design ideas.
- Give them a circular piece of paper, a pencil, ruler and any geometric shapes they need for the

design they have chosen to make from their rough sketches. Check that their design is symmetrical.
- Suggest they draw their design faintly at first in pencil to make it easier to make changes if necessary.
- Once their design is complete they need to draw on top of the pencil marks with a black felt tip pen - a ruler would be useful to help with the straight lines.
- The shapes now need colouring using the wax crayons. Tell the children to press on firmly in order to create bright, strong colours inside the shapes and not to go over the lines.
- Remind them to use the same colour for identical shapes to make sure the completed pattern is symmetrical.

Display

The designs could be individually mounted on black paper circles leaving only a small black border showing around each one. They could be arranged in circular bands around information about Mandalas and photographs of the children drawing.

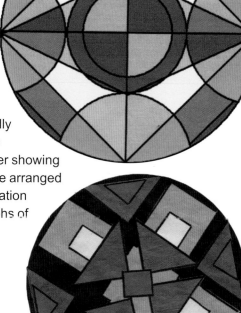

Carpets and Kilim Rugs from Turkey

These knotted carpets and flat woven rugs made of wool, cotton and sometimes silk, have large bold abstract designs on them. They have been made in Turkey for many, many years and used as blankets, curtains, covers over sofas and cushion covers, as well as on the floor. The colours used are significant - red is the colour of enthusiasm, courage, faith, luck and joy as well as sorrow and calamity. Orange stands for humility and piety. Blue symbolizes power and strength and green, which is used sparingly and only in places which are unlikely to be trodden on means hope, life, renewal and spring. Turkish mosques are often covered from wall to wall with several layers of carpet many of them given by Muslim worshippers.

Equipment Needed

Rectangles of squared maths paper (20x15cm approx.), pencils, felt tip pens and examples of Turkish carpet and rug designs from books and the Internet.

Talk About

- Where Turkey is on a map of the world and what a mosque is.
- The colours and shapes in the patterns on the rugs and carpets.
- Using the grid on the maths paper to draw the outline of different shapes. (see illustration)
- Beginning the design by drawing shapes in the middle of the paper similar to those seen in the examples. Surround them with further shapes of different sizes, some inside or joined on to others in the design.
- Filling in the shapes using felt tip pens, matching the colours seen in the examples of rugs and carpets.

Doing

- The children find the centre of a rectangle of squared paper and begin drawing their first shape around it in pencil. They add further shapes around this until they reach the edge of the paper. Remind them to keep the pattern symmetrical and to draw shapes of different sizes. Encourage the children to draw faintly with pencil at first so that it is easier to make alterations if needed.
- When the design is drawn they can find the appropriate colours of felt tip pens to fill in the shapes. Remind them to use the same colours for matching shapes and to take care to keep inside the shapes as they colour. Finally they outline the edges of any shapes that need neatening with the colour they have used.

Display

Mount the pieces of work individually on rectangles of black paper, cutting a fringe at the end of each one to make them 'rug like' and arrange them in rows.

Patterns from Persia

Textiles from Persia - now known as Iran - were originally plain. Nowadays however they feature trees, flowers, fruit, birds and animals printed, embroidered or woven onto or into them. Patterns either surround a central motif or are an all over design. When the Muslim religion (Islam) spread to Persia the designs began to change as the prophet Mohammed set out to destroy the worship of idols and forbade the Muslims to draw, carve, paint or embroider likenesses of any living thing. Artists and weavers got round this by changing and altering the motifs they used so that they became decorative and no longer true to life e.g. they would draw a bird's head on backwards.

Equipment Needed

Squares of coloured paper 10 x 10 cm approx., coloured felt tip pens, thin wax crayons, oil pastels, drawing pencils, glue and pieces of floral patterned paper - wrapping paper is ideal. Examples of Persian patterns from books and the Internet.

Talk About

- Where Iran is on a map of the world.
- How the patterns are arranged - as an all-over pattern or as a pattern with a central motif and a border.
- Choosing a piece of patterned paper to use as part of an all over pattern or as a central motif.
- Looking carefully at the colours and shapes on it that will need to be matched and added to.
- Sketching the pattern faintly in pencil first.
- Finding colours that match the patterned paper in crayons or felt tip pens.
- Finding a matching colour of background paper.
- Filling in the drawn shapes carefully.

Doing

- Once the children have chosen a piece of patterned paper they need to stick it in the middle of the coloured square that is to be the background. Make sure that the piece they choose matches the background of the printed piece.
- They need to decide what sort of pattern they are going to make. If it is an all-over pattern they begin drawing, in pencil, shapes that match and extend the design to cover and fill all the paper. If it is a pattern with a central motif, the children

draw a border around the edge of the background paper. It should contain designs that match the central motif.
- When the drawn pattern is complete the shapes will need to be filled with colours that match as closely as possible the colours on the original patterned paper, using either wax crayons, felt tip pens or oil pastels.

Display

Mount the pieces of work individually and arrange them in rows around pictures of Iran taken from travel brochures and photographs of the children working on their patterns.

Islamic Tiles

Followers of the Islamic religion, Muslims, are to be found in many parts of the world e.g. Iran, Turkey, India, and parts of Africa, as well as in the western world. Muslims

worship in mosques which are buildings usually featuring domes, minarets and courtyards. Mosques are decorated with mosaics and tiles that make detailed and intricate geometric patterns full of circles, triangles, stars etc. which represent a spiritual vision of the world and a reminder of the unity of God. The Qur'an condemns idolatry, nothing should come between a Muslim at prayer and God. God cannot be represented visually - to do so is to limit him - and as man is made in the image of God to imitate his form is tantamount to blasphemy.

Equipment Needed

White paper cut into star and hexagon shapes approx. 16 cm diameter, narrow strips of paper in a variety of shades of blue foil, glue, scissors, blue felt tip pens, pieces of scrap paper and examples of Islamic tile patterns from books and the Internet.

Talk About

- Where the main Muslim countries are in the Middle and Far East.
- Where we see and use tiles for decoration - floors, porches, walls etc. - and the sort of patterns on them.
- What a pattern is and how tiles fit together to form a pattern, sometimes with a border.
- Different lines and shapes that can be used to make a pattern e.g. spirals, dots, squares etc.
- Drawing different sorts of patterns on scrap paper using felt tip pens.
- The names of the tile shapes they are going to decorate.

Doing

- The children choose a tile shape. They also need to get glue and several strips of different shades of blue.
- They arrange the strips randomly across their tile leaving gaps between the strips. When they are happy with their arrangement thay can stick it in place.
- Any pieces of the strips that extend over the edge of the tile can be cut off accurately by turning the tile over before trimming them to the edge of the tile shape.
- Using the patterns drawn on the scrap paper for reference the children now need to draw patterns in the gaps between the blue strips using felt tip pens in different shades of blue.
- Encourage them to use many different patterns and not to fill each gap with the same sort of pattern.

Display

Cut a large shape of an Islamic arch or mosque out of black paper and place it in the centre of a board backed in blue. Arrange the completed tiles on this silhouette to decorate it. Other decorated tiles could be used to create a border around the edge of the board. Information and pictures about Islam, Mosques and Islamic tile patterns could be displayed under or next to the display.

Textiles from Thailand

The focus for textiles is on the hill tribes of the North of Thailand, the Karen, Hmong, Mien, Lahu, Lisu and Akha - who produce silk. The soil is ideally suited to the cultivation of mulberry bushes which are the main diet of the silkworm. The hill tribes also grow cotton. Each tribe has its preferred technique for decorating cloth by weaving, dyeing, stitching, batik and appliqué often in geometric patterns. The fabrics are made into clothing traditionally representing the tribe, village and status of the wearer. Such traditions are still in evidence today though mainly for the appreciation of the tourist market. Textile skills in the past were the means by which women were judged as to their suitability as prospective brides.

Equipment Needed

Coloured paper A4 size, scissors, glue, black felt tip pens, small squares of paper in a variety of sizes and colours, examples of geometrical Thai textile patterns from books and the Internet.

Talk About

- Where Thailand is on a map of the world.
- How the geometric shapes in the patterns fit together - often in rows.
- How small shapes are used on top of larger shapes to decorate them.
- How to cut diagonally across a square shape to make two triangles.
- How to make these triangles smaller by folding them in half and then cutting along the fold.
- How to make multi-coloured squares using four triangles of different colours.
- Arranging and sticking the shapes in rows across the A4 paper.
- Drawing lines across or between the shapes as part of the pattern using a felt tip pen and a ruler.

Doing

- Let the children choose a piece of A4 paper and a selection of coloured squares.
- They can cut some into smaller shapes and arrange the squares, in rows across the A4 paper making sure each shape touches its neighbour.
- When they are happy with their arrangement they can stick it down and then

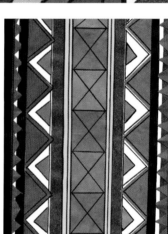

decide whether to add further smaller shapes, between or on top of those in their pattern, to make it more interesting and colourful.
- Finally using a black felt tip pen and a ruler they draw lines to outline and link the shapes together.

Display

Mount each of the patterns individually on black paper. Put a small map of the world with Thailand outlined on it and arrange the patterns in equally spaced rows above, below and around it. Make a collection of travel brochures that feature Thailand and place them near the display together with books or articles from the Internet about the country.

Chinese Dragon Designs

Dragons are said to be the combination of several different animals including the wings of a bird, the scales of a snake, the head of a camel, the paws of a tiger and the horns of a deer. In China dragons are symbols of the natural world, having great power and representing strength, adaptability, and vitality. They are credited with transporting humans to the celestial realms after death. Chinese emperors think that they are the real dragons and their people are descendants of the dragon, thus the beds the emperors sleep on are called dragon beds, the throne is called the dragon seat and their ceremonial clothes are called the dragon robes. As well as a symbol used to decorate Chinese textiles and pottery, dragons feature in traditional dances and even special boat races.

Equipment Needed

Pieces of white card, scissors, pencils, scrap paper, glue, red and black felt tip pens, coloured paper, A4 coloured card, paint and cotton wool buds. Pictures of Chinese dragon designs from books and the Internet.

Talk About

*   Where China is on a map of the world.
*   What the dragons look like in the pictures - the shape of their heads, bodies, tails, legs etc.
*   Stories they know that feature dragons.
*   Drawing heads, legs, tails and bodies for a dragon in pencil on scrap paper before choosing which ones to combine and use for the outline of a whole dragon on a piece of white card.
*   Cutting out their dragon shape and placing it on coloured card to use as a template to draw round.
*   Adding details e.g. scales, eyes, teeth etc. using a black felt tip pen.
*   Tearing thin strips from coloured paper.
*   Printing dots with a cotton wool bud dipped in paint.

Doing

*   The children make their rough sketches on scrap paper and then draw a complete dragon outline on white card.
*   They cut it out carefully and place their dragon shape on the coloured card they have chosen as a background.
*   They may want to try the outline on different parts of

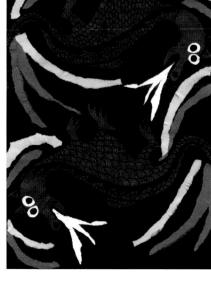

the card before they trace round it in pencil. They may want to arrange it so that they can draw several dragons on the same piece of card.

*   The children draw over the dragon outlines using red and black felt tip pens and add details such as scales, eyes, teeth etc.
*   Decoration around the dragon shapes could be added either with a cotton bud dipped in paint or torn strips of coloured paper which are then glued down.

Display

Information about dragons and pictures of dragons could be displayed as a block in the middle of the board surrounded by the individual pieces of work, each mounted on black and arranged in equally spaced rows. Travel brochures about China and stories about dragons could be added next to or under the display.

Chinese Lattice Work

More than three thousand years ago the Chinese began using wooden lattice designs in their windows. The smooth inside of the lattice was traditionally covered with rice paper creating a serene and peaceful atmosphere. This paper was replaced each year on New Year's Day signifying a fresh new start. In ancient times the architecture of a house told much about the owner's status and wealth hence great detail was paid to its decoration. Traditional Chinese doors and windows displayed a wide range of lattice work motifs to reflect Chinese philosophy on the harmony between man and nature. Many were derived from traditional designs with special meanings e.g. storks and deer symbolizing longevity and good health, arabesques (a design of flowing lines) symbolizing happiness etc. Simple and graceful geometric symbols and patterns were also popular.

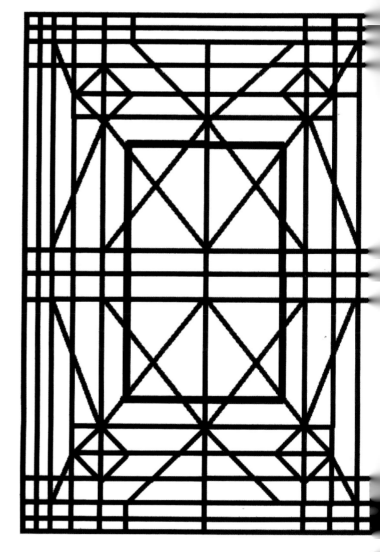

Equipment Needed

Pre-cut thin strips of black paper, dot lattice grid maths paper, glue, glue spreaders and scissors. Examples of Chinese Lattice work from books and the Internet.

Talk About

*   Where China is on a map of the world.
*   The different shapes of doors and windows found on houses in the locality plus those found on important buildings e.g. the town hall, a church etc.
*   What a geometric pattern is.
*   Making a geometric pattern using cut paper strips.
*   The arrangement of the dots on the dot lattice grid paper.
*   Using the rows of dots as a guide to help keep the pattern regular and geometric.
*   Folding and cutting strips to make them smaller but still of equal size for parts of the pattern if needed.
*   Sticking the strips down, how much glue to use and where to put it.

Doing

*   Give the children several strips of black paper and tell them to arrange them on the work surface to make a pattern, as though for a window or a door.
*   When they have experimented with several patterns give them a piece of dot lattice grid paper. Suggest that when they arrange the strips to make their next pattern, they use the rows of dots to help them keep the lines straight, and to create squares, rectangles and diagonals.

*   Remind them that they can fold some of the strips and cut them to make shorter or thinner pieces if needed.
*   When they are happy with their pattern and are sure that it is made up of geometric shapes, they stick the strips down carefully.

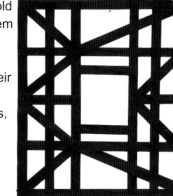

Display

Back the board in red and cut pictures of old ornate Chinese buildings from travel brochures etc. Arrange these in the middle of the board. Use strips of black paper to create a grid shape around them. Mount the individual pieces of work on black and arrange them in equally spaced rows around the grid in the centre.

Japanese Stencils

Japanese paper stencil patterns were first used for applying designs in dye to leather goods such as stirrups and warrior helmets. As the wearing of kimonos (The traditional T-shaped dress) became popular, stencils came to be used for dying textiles. Japanese stencils are themselves considered works of art and are collected and valued. They are made from sheets of hand made mulberry paper glued together and are cut using special tools. Stencil cutters are highly skilled and have been designated 'Living National Treasures' by the government. When the stencils are placed on fabric, rice paste resist is applied. Later the stencils are removed and the fabric dyed. The paste is removed by washing the fabric revealing the stencil patterns.

Equipment Needed

White cotton fabric, squares of sticky backed plastic (10 x 10 cm approx.), pencils, scissors and fabric crayons. Examples of ready cut stencils - most DIY shops have these.

Talk About

- Where Japan is in the world.
- What a Kimono is and what it looks like.
- What a stencil is and how it is made. Looking at and feeling the shapes cut from the example stencils.
- Where they have seen stencils and what they are used to decorate.
- Simple outlines that would be suitable as stencils e.g. flowers, fish, leaves, butterflies etc.
- Drawing the outline of a shape in pencil on the back of the sticky backed plastic.
- Cutting this shape out before removing the backing from the plastic.
- Placing the cut stencil carefully on to fabric, sticky side down.
- Colouring inside the cut shape using fabric crayons.

Doing

- The children could practise creating shapes on scrap paper.
- The children draw their shape in pencil on the back of their sticky backed plastic. They cut this shape out carefully keeping the area around the cut shape intact (see examples on the right).
- They peel the back from the sticky back plastic and place their stencil on to fabric, sticky side down, and press it into place.
- They next colour inside the cut out part of the stencil

Flower stencil

using a fabric crayon. The stencil can then be removed and placed on a different part of the fabric and the process repeated. This could be done several times to continue the design and cover the fabric.
- Finally details could be added to the design, in between and around the motifs, by freely drawing with fabric crayons.

Display

Display the examples of pre-cut stencils and pictures of stencilled objects in the middle of the board. Then write descriptions of how they made their stencils. These could be mounted along with their work and arranged in equally spaced rows around the examples.

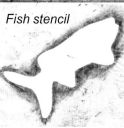
Fish stencil

Japanese Heraldic Crests

The tradition of choosing or giving family crests developed among the nobility around 800 -1200 AD. This was a time of peace and the motifs used were often poetic and symbolic e.g. flowers, fruit, leaves etc. Sometimes the subject was related to an occupation or possession, or to commemorate a special event which brought honour to the family, or to preserve the memory of a special or famous ancestor. Later every Samurai family had a crest and only they, the imperial family and lords, were allowed to use them. Their crests appeared on their banners, clothing and swords. Eventually restrictions were lifted and wealthy merchants began using crests many of which today have become corporate symbols. Commoners started wearing crests too e.g. on formal kimonos. Women usually use the crest of their husband's family when they marry. Crests continue to be used on lanterns and doors to show ownership as well as on the roof tiles of temples, on shopping bags, advertisements and even jewellery.

Equipment Needed

Black and white paper A4 size and also 20 x 20 cm squares, pencils, scissors, glue, black and white paint, pieces of card to be used as palettes and fine paintbrushes. Examples of Japanese Crests and Coats of Arms in books and from the Internet, also carrier bags that show the logos of familiar shops.

Talk About

- Where Japan is on a map of the world.
- The pictures of the coats of arms, the families they belong to and what the symbols are and what they might represent.
- The logos on the carrier bags and what they tell us.
- The motifs found on Japanese crests.
- The shapes they might use on a crest for different professions e.g. an artist, a dentist, a plumber etc. or for a celebrity e.g. a pop star, a footballer or author etc.

- The shapes they might use on a crest for themselves or their family and what the chosen shapes might mean.
- Drawing and cutting shapes out of black and white paper.
- Arranging and gluing shapes on a background.
- Drawing with a fine paint brush.

Doing

- Let the children sketch designs on scrap paper choosing their preferred crest.
- Ask the children to choose either a black or white square as their background and then to sketch the shapes for their crest on a piece of paper in the opposite colour.
- Remind them that these shapes must fit on and fill the background paper.
- Once the shapes are cut out they need to be glued to the background paper and further details added using paint and a fine paint brush.

Display

Mount the work on black or white squares and arrange them in rows around a block of written work in which the children describe the design for their crests or those for a celebrity or a profession.

Tapa Cloth from Fiji

Tapa cloth is made from mulberry bark. Strips of it are dried, soaked and pounded until they become wide and flexible before being felted together to form cloth. This is then painted and decorated with home made dyes. The brown shade is made from tree bark, black from burnt candle nuts and red from red clay. The light

area is the unpainted fibre. Tapa cloth is flimsy and loses its strength when wet. It was primarily used for clothing although nowadays it has been replaced by cotton and other textiles. It is still often worn on formal occasions such as weddings and funerals. It is also prized for its decorative value and often found hanging on walls. Different Fijian Islands have their own distinctive patterns.

Equipment Needed

Circles of brown paper 17 cm in diameter approx., paper strips of cream and a different shade of brown approx. 6 cm wide, scissors, glue, brown paint, black paint, thin strips of card and cotton buds plus pieces of card to use as palettes. Pictures of Tapa cloth from books and the Internet.

Talk About

- Where the Pacific Ocean is and where Fiji is on a map of the world.
- The colours and patterns on the Tapa cloth.
- Folding strips of paper in half and then in half again before cutting shapes from the top and bottom of the folded strip.
- Cutting further shapes from both edges of the strip making sure a hinge is left to keep the strip in one piece.
- Opening the strip to reveal a repeating pattern and then arranging and sticking this strip across a circle.

- Printing lines and dots with thin strips of card and cotton buds by dipping them in paint before pressing them on to paper and lifting them off to reveal the marks.

Doing

- Let the children choose several of the cut paper strips, and fold them lengthwise twice and then to cut repeating shapes out of them, remembering to leave a hinge at each side so that the strip remains intact when it is opened up.

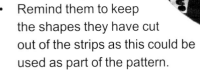

- Remind them to keep the shapes they have cut out of the strips as this could be used as part of the pattern.
- When they have cut several patterned strips they arrange the opened strips across a brown paper circle with spaces between each one, before gluing them down.
- Finally they add further decoration by printing with the thin strips of card and cotton buds dipped in paint.

Display

Put a world map with Fiji marked in the middle of the board and arrange the decorated circles, equally spaced, in a circle around it. Use further circles around the edge of this circle following the curved shape. Travel brochures about the Pacific Islands could be arranged down the edges of the board or under it.

Patterns from the Pacific

Patchwork from Hawaii - Tivaivai

Tivaivai quilts are sewn by women in Hawaii, Tahiti and the Cook Islands. It is uncertain when quilting began in the Pacific but it is known that missionary wives and Chinese sailors played an instrumental role in the introduction of quilting techniques. Tivaivai quilts are large and brightly coloured often featuring repeating patterns of local flowers, fruit and plants decorated by painting, sewing or stencilling. They are not usually displayed in the house but are folded up and hidden from view for most of their existence. Quilts tend to be passed down through the family and become family heirlooms.

Equipment Needed

A4 paper in bright colours, felt tip pens, scissors, pencils, scrap paper and glue. Pictures of quilts from Hawaii in books and from the Internet. Brightly coloured flowers and different leaf shapes as a stimulus.

Talk About

- Where the Pacific Ocean is and where Hawaii is on a map of the world.
- The motifs used to make the patterns on the examples of the quilts.
- The shapes, sizes and colours of the motifs and how they fit together to make a repeating pattern.
- The shapes of the different flowers and leaves on the stimulus material.
- Folding a piece of scrap paper over several times before drawing the outline of a flower and or a leaf shape either from observation or imagination on the top surface.
- Cutting the shape out carefully whilst the paper is folded to produce several copies of the same shape.
- Arranging the shapes to make a repeating pattern.
- Adding decoration and detail to these shapes by drawing with a felt tip pen.

Doing

- When the children have sketched the outline of several leaf and/or flower shapes on scrap paper they can decide which ones they are going to use.
- Using brightly coloured paper, they fold it several times and draw their chosen shape lightly in pencil on the top surface.
- If they are going to combine several shapes in their pattern each one will need to be drawn on a different colour of paper, folded as before.
- These shapes are cut out carefully and arranged to form a repeating pattern on a piece of A4 paper. This becomes the background.
- When they are happy with their arrangement it needs to be stuck down. Outlines and details are added to the shapes using felt tip pens.

Display

Mount each of the quilt designs on black paper and arrange them in equally spaced rows around a map of the world with Hawaii marked on it. Add pictures of Hawaii cut from travel brochures or downloaded from the Internet. Keep the spaces between the pieces of work to a minimum for maximum impact.

42

Aboriginal Designs from Australia

In place of a written language the symbols in Aboriginal artwork tell stories about their past - The Dreamtime. The Dreamtime is the name given to the time when the world was created. Aborigines believe ancestral beings rose out of the earth and journeyed across the land shaping it and laying down rules about how people should behave. When the Dreamtime ended, these beings disappeared, or remained on earth as natural features such as mountains, streams and valleys. Aboriginal symbols used in paintings often have several meanings even within the same picture e.g. a series of concentric circles can mean a waterhole, a campfire, a mountain or a tree. The interpretation of each picture depends on several things; the knowledge of the artist, who must only paint Dreamings (symbols) of which their particular family has ownership; the viewer; and an understanding of the past. The dots surrounding the symbols are in fact a form of camouflage.

Equipment Needed

Brown paper squares 21 x 21 cm approx., cotton buds, white oil pastel crayons, brown, yellow, white, black and red paint, pieces of card as palettes and examples of Aboriginal Art plus some of the symbols and their meaning.

Talk About

*   Where Australia is on a map of the world.
*   Symbols we see and are familiar with in our world today.
*   The symbols in the Aboriginal pictures and what they might mean.
*   Drawing with an oil pastel crayon and printing with cotton buds dipped in paint.

Doing

*   Ask the children to choose an Aboriginal symbol and to draw it boldly in white oil pastel in the middle of a brown paper square.
*   After looking at the patterns made by dots in the Aboriginal paintings they need to print and add similar patterns around their drawn symbol using cotton buds dipped in the different colours of paint.

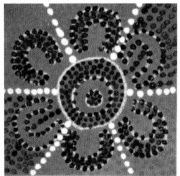

Display

Cut the silhouette of the shape of Australia out of black paper and arrange it in the middle of a board backed in brown. Mount the individual pieces of work on black paper and arrange them in equally spaced rows around the silhouette. Display travel brochures and books about Australia next to or beneath the display.

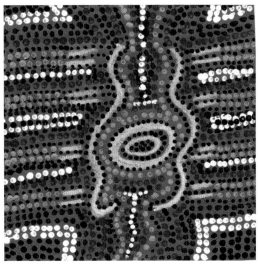

Australian Bark Painting

Bark painting is an Australian Aboriginal art-form which is created on the inside of strips of tree bark. The bark chosen must be free of knots and other blemishes and is best cut in the wet season when the sap is rising. The bark is first placed in a fire before being flattened under foot and weighted with stones or logs to dry flat. Earth colours such as red, yellow, black and white are used and the completed work fixed with a binder e.g. sap or the juice of plants such as orchid bulbs. Bark paintings were traditionally produced for ceremonies or as a means of instruction. Now they are keenly sought after by collectors and galleries.

Equipment Needed

Pieces of white card 15 x 15 cm approx., wax crayons, plastic knives or wooden spatulas, pieces of bark, pictures of animals native to Australia and examples of Australian bark paintings from books and the Internet.

Talk About

*   Where Australia is on a map of the world and the different sorts of animals in the pictures and what they are called.
*   What the pieces of bark look like and feel like.
*   Covering a piece of card with patches of different colours - but not black - using wax crayons.
*   Colouring over and covering the coloured patches using a black wax crayon.
*   Making a drawing by pressing and scratching into the black wax covering using a spatula or a plastic knife.
*   Revealing some of the colours under the black but leaving some of the black intact. This way of working is called scraffito.

Doing

*   Allow the children to sketch some of the Australian animals on a scrap of paper to help them choose which animals to use in their designs.
*   Cover pieces of white card with patches of colour using the wax crayons, remembering to press on firmly to get a rich covering of each colour.
*   When the card is covered they crayon over the colour using a black wax crayon. Remind them again to press on firmly to get a rich covering and to hide all the patches of colour below.
*   They draw their chosen animal using either a plastic knife or a wooden spatula. Encourage them to first draw the outline shape of their animal and to scrape away and remove the excess black wax to reveal colour underneath. They can continue to add detail to their animal with further scratching and drawing into the black wax until the design is complete.
*   Finally patterns or shapes could be drawn in the same way to surround the animal.

Display

Back the diplay board in black and put a world map showing Australia in the middle. Mount the pieces of work individually on red or brown paper and display them in equally spaced rows.

Maori Tattoos - Moko

Moko is the name for the tattoos that decorate the faces, hands and body parts of the Maori people of New Zealand. The full-face Moko was a mark of distinction for Maori men as it told of their status, family or tribe and important events in their lives. The head was considered the most important part of the body. All high ranking Maori were tattooed and those who went without tattoos were seen as persons of no social status. The Moko was created by literally carving the skin with a chisel. Natural pigments - and even gunpowder were then added to the skin to accentuate the intricate spiral patterns. Women also wore moko usually on their chin to mark their passage into adulthood, commemorate a special occasion and to beautify themselves.

Equipment Needed

Brown sugar paper A4 size cut into face shapes, black wax crayons or black oil pastels, scrap paper, scissors and pictures of tattooed Maori faces from books and the Internet.

Talk About

*   The Maori people.
*   Where New Zealand is on a map of the world.
*   How we decorate our faces nowadays e.g. using face paints to show which football team we support, and how celebrities sport tattoos e.g. film stars, pop stars, sports stars.
*   Drawing curves and spirals on scrap paper using black crayons or oil pastels.
*   Folding a piece of paper in half so that the opposite edges are touching and cutting shapes out of a piece of paper whilst it is folded so that two identical shapes are cut at the same time.

Doing

*   The children practise drawing curves and spirals on scrap paper.
*   The children each need a brown sugar paper face shape to fold in half lengthwise. Whilst the paper is folded draw the outline shape of half a nose outwards from the fold into the middle. Cut it out. When the paper is

opened it should reveal a full nose shape.
*   Fold the paper up again and leaving a space next to the cut out nose, draw the outline shape of one eye. Cut this eye out carefully making sure that the cut goes through the top piece and the piece folded under it. Two eyes, one on either side of the nose will have been cut out and will be revealed once the paper is opened.
*   Fold the paper again. Leave a space under the nose, draw outwards from the fold line the outline shape of half a mouth and cut it out. When the paper is opened it should reveal a full mouth.

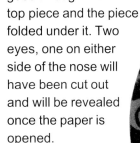

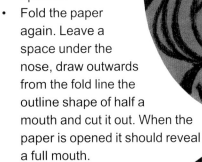

*   Once the cutting is complete the paper face needs opening and flattening before being decorated with curves and spirals in a symmetrical pattern i.e. each half of the face is decorated in the same way, using the black drawing media.

Display

Back the display board in red or cream and put a map and pictures of New Zealand in the middle. Arrange the decorated Maori faces in equally spaced rows on a red or cream background.

Koru Patterns from New Zealand

The Koru is a symbol that comes from the Maori people of New Zealand and represents a fern frond before it has unfurled. Each fern shoot has a tip, which is curled over and which will unfold to become a fern leaf. It represents growth and vitality, the unfurling of new ideas and opportunities throughout life, the search for enlightenment and a reminder that all things live, die and are reborn. It is a symbol much used in Maori art from jewellery to carved wood. As a symbol of celebration and homage it is painted in patterns called Kowhaiwhai, which are designs of interwoven Koru on tombs, monuments and the rafters of meeting houses. Such Koru are almost invariably painted white and the surrounding space blocked in or stippled in red or black.

Equipment Needed

Strips of red and black paper 10 x 30 cm approx., pieces of white paper, pencils, scrap paper, scissors, glue, black felt tip pens, pictures of fern fronds and Koru patterns from books and the Internet.

Talk About

*   The Maori people
*   Where New Zealand is on a map of the world.
*   What a meeting house would be used for and the places that we use to hold meetings.
*   The shape of the fern fronds in the picture and how they are similar to the Koru shapes in the patterns.
*   What an outline is and drawing the outline of spiral shapes in pencil on scrap paper.
*   Cutting these shapes out carefully and arranging them to form an interlocking pattern.
*   Drawing with a felt tip pen.

Doing

*   Let the children practise drawing spiral shapes on scrap paper.
*   Give the children a piece of white paper. Fold it over several times before drawing a spiral shape on the top surface in pencil.
*   Keeping the paper folded, this shape needs to be cut out carefully. Several versions of the same shape will emerge.

*   The children use a strip of red or black paper and arrange their cut out spirals on it to make an interlocking pattern.
*   They may need to draw and cut extra spirals in the same way to complete their pattern.
*   Once they are happy with their arrangement they stick it down carefully.
*   Finally the spiral shapes need to be outlined in black felt tip pen to give them greater impact.

Display

Cut the silhouette of the gabled end of a house out of black paper and on it arrange pictures of Maori meeting houses and scenes of New Zealand cut from travel brochures. Use the un-mounted Koru patterns in lines that follow the outline of the house.

Patchwork Quilts

The early American settlers were very practical. When they needed warm bed covers for the cold winter nights, the women made them by piecing and stitching together pieces of material from garments that were no longer needed. They used their imaginative and artistic talents to create fascinating designs, frequently developed from triangles, squares and diamonds. Making patchwork quilts was such a popular pastime that it became a social occasion. 'Quilting bees' were held when a group of women met at one person's house to gossip whilst each stitched her own individual block of patchwork. Eventually all the completed blocks would be joined together to make a full sized bed cover. Traditional patchwork designs have names e.g. Nine Patch, Log Cabin, Saw Tooth, Lazy Rose.

Equipment Needed

Small squares of coloured paper and wrapping paper, A4 coloured paper as a background, scissors, rulers, glue, black felt tip pens, examples of patchwork designs from books and the Internet.

Talk About

- What patchwork is.
- Where North America is on a world map.
- The shapes that make up the patterns in the picture, how they are repeated and fit together. How colours and patterned pieces are also repeated in the designs.
- Drawing diagonally across a square to divide it into two triangles and then cutting along the line.

- Positioning squares so that they look like diamonds and placing smaller shapes between and on top of larger shapes to make a pattern.
- Using patterned and plain pieces together in a design.
- Making sure the colours and shapes chosen repeat throughout the pattern.

Doing

- Once the children have chosen the coloured squares they want to use they decide which ones to cut and which ones to leave intact, before arranging them to make a repeating pattern on a coloured piece of A4 paper.
- They may try several arrangements before they are happy with their pattern and are ready to stick it down.
- Lines to link and outline some of the shapes could then be added using rulers and black felt tip pens.
- Further patchwork designs could be produced by drawing on squared paper and using felt-tip pens to colour them, or by using a computer graphics programme. Dazzle and its tile facility have been used here.

Display

Mount the completed pieces of work individually. Arrange them in equally spaced rows with small gaps between each piece around a central block of pictures and information about patchwork quilts and a map of North America.

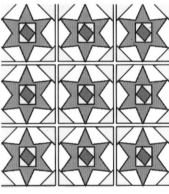

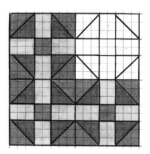

Totem Poles

The Red Indian tribes of the North West coast of America were the makers of the tall brightly painted totem poles carved from red cedar. The poles were made up of symbols relating to a family rather like a coat of arms. The owner's personal crest was usually placed at the top and each of the lower layers represented ancestors of his wife and details of family history. These crests often represented legendary encounters between an ancestor and the spirits of the sea, sky, river, forest and mountains. Some of the creatures carved were e.g. the killer whale - believed to be a race of transformed men (it represents beauty and power) - the wolf, respected as a good hunter (it represents intelligence and leadership) - the bear, believed to have abducted and married an Indian girl (it represents strength, humility and motherhood) - the beaver, because like the Indians it cut down trees and made traps for fishing (it represents resoucefulness and creativity) - the raven, believed to have created the world and was a great trickster (it represents honour, power and wisdom).Totem poles proclaim ownership of land and property and the status and privilege of the family. They are considered to have spiritual powers because of the mystical animals carved on them.

Equipment Needed

Pieces of white paper 30 cm x 13 cm approx., white, red, yellow and black paper, glue, pencils, scissors, black felt tip pens plus pictures of totem poles in books and from the Internet.

Talk About

* Where North America is.
* What totem poles are.
* What a coat of arms is, and who has them.
* The symbols that the children think would best represent their family.
* The shape and colours of the totem poles in the pictures plus the animals and birds on them, how they fit together and the patterns decorating them.

* Drawing the outline of strange animals and birds in pencil then cutting these shapes out and adding decoration to them with other colours and black felt tip pens.

Doing

* Let the children experiment with drawing strange 'totem' figures on scrap paper.
* When the children have chosen different colours of paper they draw the outline of an animal or bird - strange and imaginary ones would be best - on each piece.
* They cut out these shapes and arrange them so that they fit together, totem pole style down the length of a piece of white paper.
* They may need to enlarge, reduce or add to their shapes, to build them into a pole shape before gluing them down.
* Each animal and bird shape needs to be decorated and have features added using cut paper shapes and drawing, using black felt tip pens.

Display

Back the board in red and individually mount the pieces of work on black. Put a block of information about totem poles in the middle of the board. Arrange the mounted pieces of work in groups in vertical lines like totem poles beside, above and below the information.

Navajo Rugs

The Navajo people of Eastern Arizona gained fame as weavers of beautiful bold patterns on blankets which were worn as shawls or used as rugs. Many of the patterns they used were similar to those of their neighbours, the Pueblo people, in New Mexico. The most common shapes used in the designs are angular lines, zig zags, rows of diamonds, crosses and stepped designs. Although these are abstract shapes they actually reflect myths and practices with spiritual significance to the Navajo. The patterns are usually based on stripes in browns, beige, yellow, indigo, black and deep red.

Equipment Needed

Pieces of red, brown and white paper 21 x14 cm approx., pieces, strips and small squares of red, white, yellow, brown and black paper, pencils, squared paper, scissors, glue and pictures of Navajo rugs from books and the Internet.

Talk About

- Where Arizona is on a map of North America.
- The patterns on rugs children have at home and the colours and patterns on the rugs in the pictures.
- The names of the shapes used in the patterns and how they are arranged.
- Drawing similar shapes in the air with a finger before drawing them in pencil on squared paper and finally drawing them on the pieces of coloured paper.
- Cutting these shapes out and arranging them on a background.
- Cutting and adding smaller shapes in different colours between and on top of the large shapes.
- What a border pattern is, where it goes, how it is a repetition of similar shapes and the sort of shapes to use for the borders of their design.

Doing

- When the children are confident in drawing the different abstract shapes on squared paper they choose different colours and shapes of paper, draw the shapes on them and cut them out.
- They choose a piece of coloured paper as the background and arrange their shapes on it. Remind them to leave room for a border either at each end or all the way round.
- When they are happy with their arrangement they glue it down. They can cut and add further shapes to decorate their design. Then cut several shapes of similar size and colour to use and arrange as the border.

Display

Mount each of the pieces of work individually on rectangles of black paper and cut a fringe in each end to represent a rug. Back the board in red, cut the silhouette of a rug out of black paper and place it in the middle of the board. Put the title of the display on this. Arrange the individual rugs in equally spaced rows around it. Leave fairly small spaces between the pieces of work for maximum impact.

Sand Paintings

The Hopi and Navajo people of Arizona are known for paintings in the sand using carefully gathered and prepared pigments of mainly white, blue, yellow and black which are linked to four sacred mountains and their direction - Arizona's San Francisco Peaks (West), Navajo Mountain in Utah (North), Mt. Blanco in Colorado (East) and Mt. Taylor in New Mexico (South). The Navajo name for sand painting is 'iikaah' which means a place where gods come and go because these paintings are of sacred importance. They also celebrate important events e.g. a new home, a new baby, and are a cure for ills. A medicine man begins the sand painting ritual and as most sand paintings are between six and eight feet, several men and women are needed to complete it. The work begins at the centre and must face east. The designs are usually abstract representations of the sun, stars, birds, snakes, arrows, turtles, frogs, feathers etc. Birds are believed to carry prayers to heaven. An ill patient would be seated in the centre of the sand painting as the medicine man performs his ritual. When it is completed the coloured sands would be swept away and either buried or scattered to the four points of the compass.

Equipment Needed

Pieces of brown sugar paper 18 x 20 cm approx., yellow, black, white and turquoise paint, pieces of card to use as palettes, small pieces of sponge, cotton buds, white chalk, pencils and scrap paper and black felt tip pens plus examples of sand paintings in books and from the Internet.

Talk About

- Where Arizona and Utah are on a map of North America.
- The colours and shapes found in the paintings.
- Drawing and dabbing with sponge to give the idea of the texture of sand.
- Printing with a cotton bud dipped in paint.
- Adding outlines and final details by drawing with a felt tip pen.
- Sketching ideas for a design on scrap paper in pencil.

Doing

- Once the children have got their piece of brown paper, paint and sponge they need to draw in white chalk, the outline of the main shapes in their design.
- These shapes are filled using the sponge and the remaining colours. Encourage the children to dab as they fill in the shapes rather than smear to retain the texture of sand.
- Patterns and further details can then be added using the cotton buds dipped in paint.
- Finally outlines and other details can be drawn in using black felt tip pens.

Display

Back the board in turquoise and mount the individual pieces of work on black. Arrange pictures and information about sand paintings together with pictures of the children making their paintings as a block in the middle of the board. Surround this block with equally spaced rows of work. Leave a wider gap between the work and the central block than between the individual pieces of work, which need to be close together with only a narrow gap between them for maximum impact.

Beadwork Belts

The Crow and Iroquois Indians of the Northern plains were famous for their beadwork which decorated bags, pouches and belts. Initially the Indians made beads by carving them from clam shells. Most of these were white but some were mauve and these were considered very precious. Such beads were known as wampum and were used as currency, and to convey messages. Glass beads were introduced into the Americas by Christopher Columbus. They were mostly made in Venice. Beads became a standard trade item between Indians and white men and also within Indian groups. Common colours used were red, yellow, green, dark and light blue and white. The Indians used these to decorate leather by sewing the bright coloured beads on to it in symmetrical patterns involving diagonal lines, circles, squares, triangles and diamond shapes.

Equipment Needed

Pieces of grey sugar paper 30 x13 cm approx., small squares and strips of coloured paper, glue, scissors, cotton wool buds, paint in assorted colours, pieces of card to use as palettes and pictures of Indian bead work from books and the Internet.

Talk About

*   Where the Northern plains are on a map of North America.
*   The shapes and colours used in the bead patterns.
*   What symmetry means and making symmetrical patterns in coloured pegs on a peg board.
*   Arranging cut shapes and strips to make a symmetrical pattern.
*   Cutting the shapes and strips to make them smaller to add to the pattern.
*   Printing with a cotton bud dipped in paint.

Doing

*   Let the children make symmetrical patterns using peg boards.
*   Give the children a piece of grey sugar paper and put it portrait style on the work surface. Remind them that the pattern they make needs to repeat and be symmetrical, all the way down the strip.
*   They use coloured strips and squares to arrange on their background paper. Remind them to leave gaps between some of the shapes, to be filled in later with printing.
*   To make their pattern more interesting, they could cut some shapes and strips smaller, to go on top of, or between, the larger ones.
*   Remind them that the colours, as well as the shapes they use, need to be symmetrical and repeat in the same sequence down the pattern.
*   When they are happy with their arrangement, they stick it down and fill in the gaps by printing with cotton buds dipped in paint. Once again the colours used must repeat and keep the pattern symmetrical.

Display

Mount the pieces of work individually on black and arrange them in equally spaced vertical rows down the board. Information about the beadwork can be put in the middle of the board, together with photos of the children's peg board patterns.

Mola Designs

Mola is the Cuna Indian word for their intricate appliqué needlework which has strong links with the body painting they used to practise in the past. The Cuna people are natives of Panama and the islands off the Atlantic Panamanian coast. To make a Mola, layers of rectangular pieces of coloured cotton cloth are sewn together. A design is then drawn in pencil on the top layer which is usually bright red, orange or black. The layers of fabric are then cut through and with each cut pieces of cloth are removed so that the colours of the lower layers show through. The cut edges of the cloth are then carefully folded under and finished with hidden stitches. Young girls of six or seven learn how to make a Mola so that by the time they are ready to marry they have several blouses decorated with this type of needlework. Traditional designs include religious, mythological and superstitious objects, flowers, geometric figures, insects, fish, lizards and mazes.

Equipment Needed

Squares of black paper 21 x 21cm approx., squares of brightly coloured paper, scissors, glue, black felt tip pens, pencils and examples of Mola designs in books and from the Internet.

Talk About

- Where Panama is on a map of the world.
- What appliqué means.
- The colours and shapes in the Mola designs and how they fit together in layers one on top of the other.
- Drawing the outline of a shape in pencil on a piece of coloured paper and then cutting it out and placing it on a different coloured piece of paper and drawing round it making the outline slightly bigger than the original one. Cutting out the second shape and combining it with the first by placing one on top of the other so that they appear layered like the Mola designs.
- Outlining the shapes in each layer with black felt tip pen.

Doing

- The children draw in pencil and cut out the outline of their first shape on coloured paper. They decide how many more identical shapes they need to cut in the same colour for their Mola pattern.
- They draw a larger version around their first shape and cut it out to form a second layer under the first one.

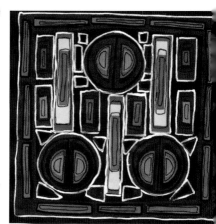

Again several of these may be needed. They can continue drawing round, enlarging and cutting out further shapes from different colours until they feel they have enough to make their pattern.

- They now arrange the shapes on a square of black paper in layers i.e. the largest shapes under the smallest ones so that each colour can be seen.
- When they are happy with their arrangement they stick it down and then outline each shape in black felt tip pen.

Display

Mount the work individually and arrange it in equally spaced rows around a world map showing Panama and pictures and information about Molas.

The Eye of God - Ojo de Dios

Thousands of years ago the Indians of Mexico and Bolivia made a good luck charm out of twigs, strips of animal skins and long plant fibres. It was called the Eye of God because the Indians believed the centre of the crossed twigs held the Eye of God and when they wanted a special favour from the gods e.g. good luck when hunting, they would ask the tribe's holy man to chant prayers whilst making a God's Eye for them. In later years when the Indians could spin and dye yarn this design was used and the Ojos became very colourful. The colours were chosen according to which god was being asked for a favour e.g. blue for rain, green for fertility, yellow for the sun etc. In Mexico when a child was born, the central eye was woven by the father, then a bit of yarn added for every year of the child's life until the child was five. In Bolivia, God's Eyes were made to be placed on an altar so that the gods could watch over the praying people and protect them.

Equipment Needed

Wooden spatulas or lolly sticks, wool in different colours, scissors, glue and examples of God's Eyes from books and the Internet.

Talk About

- Where Mexico and Bolivia are on a map of the world.
- Items that we consider to be good luck charms e.g. horseshoes, four leaf clovers etc.
- The shape and colours of the God's eyes in the pictures.
- Wrapping wool around each arm of the crossed spatulas in rotation.
- Joining different colours of wool together by knotting.

Doing

- The children each need two spatulas. Place one on top of the other to form a cross.
- They choose their first colour of wool and tie it in an X shape across the middle of the cross to fix the spatulas together.
- Now they start wrapping the wool over, then under, each arm of the cross always going in the same order until several rows are complete.
- When they want a change of colour they need to cut off the old wool and tie on a second colour before continuing to wrap the wool over and under each arm as before.
- As many colours as desired can be joined on and

added until the Ojo is complete.
- The final end of wool needs to be fastened with a blob of glue and a loop made for hanging.

Display

Put information and photographs of the children making their God's Eyes, together with instructions on how to make one, in the middle of the board. Hang the completed God's Eyes in a circular arrangement (several circles may be needed) around it. Arrange a box of spatulas and a basket of wool under the display for others to try and make a God's Eye.

Huichol Prayer Bowls - Jicaras

The Huichol Indians of Mexico have no written language, it is their art work that conveys their beliefs and traditions. To make containers for offerings to the gods they would hollow out bowls from gourds. They then spread a thin layer of resin and bees wax on to the inside and decorated them by pressing seeds, shells and stones often coloured with insect or vegetable dye into it. Significant religious designs representing health, luck, abundance and communion with the spirit world were the main theme. When the missionaries arrived from Europe they brought glass beads and their bright colours began to appear in more intricate designs. These bowls were used to make wishes for good health, a good harvest etc. or to honour a particular ancestor, object, animal or event. The Huichol believed that just as we drink water from a bowl, the gods drank up the petitions in the bowls. These bowls were left at Huichol sacred places e.g. caves, temples and paths of pilgrimage. Other Huichol art forms are yarn paintings made by pressing fibres into wax, bead jewellery and beaded bags, belts etc.

Equipment Needed

Paper bowls, cotton buds, paint in assorted colours and pieces of card to be used as palettes, pictures of Huichol prayer bowls in books and from the Internet.

Talk About

*   Where Mexico is on a map of the world.
*   The names of objects we know that are decorated with beads e.g. clothes, bracelets, children's toys etc.
*   Printing with a cotton bud dipped in paint by pressing on and lifting off.
*   Using a new cotton bud for each new colour to avoid the colours becoming dirty.

*   Working from the centre of the bottom of the bowl outwards to avoid smudging.
*   Turning the bowl whilst working to make it easier to cover all parts.

Doing

*   Give the children a bowl, a selection of different colours of paint and several cotton buds. They need to begin printing a pattern on their bowl starting at the centre and working outwards.
*   Encourage them to print each dot close to its neighbour for a rich covering of colour and to turn the bowl as they work to make it easier to work on the different parts.
*   An alternative way of adding pattern to a bowl would be by fastening strips of double sided sellotape to the bottom and sides of the bowl and then to press small plastic beads on to the sticky surface.

Display

As it is the inside of these bowls that are to be displayed, they should be attached to the board through the middle of the decorated inside with a straight pin, using a pin push. Arrange the bowls in a series of circles around photographs of the children producing their bowls plus information about prayer bowls, and a world map showing the position of Mexico.

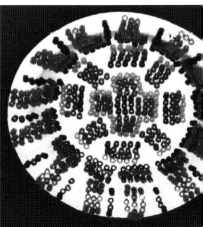

Guatemalan Textiles

Guatemala is a place where many traditional textile arts from ancient cultures survive, though nowadays modern techniques and materials have been incorporated. Mayan spinners and weavers still produce the brilliant and vivid hues and traditional motifs used by their ancestors, the patterns and colours of which reflect the village from which they come. Weaving is usually done by women on a back strap or stick loom which is portable and striped patterns are popular as they are effective and easy to weave on such looms. Other designs woven on foot - looms include diamonds, suns, moons, flowers, plants, birds, animals, crosses and zigzags. Some designs mark the passage of time e.g. when the weaver makes colour changes on the 18th, 20th, 19th, and 5th rows to make the eighteen months of twenty days and the nineteenth month of five days that make up the Mayan calendar. Weaving is associated with the gods, mainly with the moon goddess Ixchel who was believed to have invented weaving and was the patron of birth and medicine.

Equipment Needed

Pieces of grey sugar paper 11 x 25 cm approx., rulers, chalk pastels and pictures of Guatemalan textiles, particularly those with striped patterns, from books and the Internet.

Talk About

- Where Guatemala is on a map of the world.
- What spinning is and what weaving is.
- The colours in the striped patterns and how the stripes join together, repeat and are of different widths.
- What is meant by vivid colours.
- Drawing with chalk pastels, pressing on firmly for a rich covering of colour.
- Drawing along the edge of a ruler to tidy up the edges of the stripes.
- Working across from one edge to the other or from top to bottom on the paper to avoid smudging.

Doing

- The children need to cover the work surface with newspaper before they start as working in chalk pastel produces a lot of dust.
- They take a piece of grey sugar paper and place it either portrait or landscape way up depending on which way they want to work.
- They need rulers and chalk pastels in a selection of colours and to begin drawing their stripey patterns.
- Remind them to work from end to end or top to bottom to avoid smudging, to press on firmly and to blow any surplus dust on to the newspaper. The edges of each stripe can be tidied up as it is completed using a ruler

Display

The finished work will need to be 'fixed' (give each piece a squirt of hairspray) before mounting them individually on black. Arrange them as a block in the middle of the board surrounded by the title and pictures of Guatemala, Guatemalan textiles and the children drawing their patterns.

Pottery from Peru - Chulucanas Pottery

Thousands of years ago the potters of the coastal deserts of Peru were known throughout the land for their fine ceramics. They used local clay and decorated their pots with natural coloured slips (liquid clay) in earth colours. For them, making pottery was a way of communicating with the earth and giving praise to the creative gods of the universe. The decoration of their pots was based on ancient motifs. Similar pottery is still made today and the potters use only their hands and feet - no potter's wheel. The finished pieces are given a base coat of colour before being smoked twice with smouldering mango or banana leaves. The quantity of fuel used in the second firing provides the variety of shades. They are then burnished with a special polishing stone, and designs added using a paste of earth and water. The town of Chulucanas is in North West Peru.

Equipment Needed

Pieces of brown, black and grey A4 paper, strips of the same colours plus cream, pencils, scissors, glue and pictures of Chulucanas Pottery from books and the Internet.

Talk About

- Where Peru is on a map of the world.
- The shapes of the vases and pots in the pictures and the shape of vases and pots in school.
- The colours of the pots and the geometric patterns on them and how these patterns are arranged.
- How to cut zig-zags, circles, thin strips and triangles from folded strips of paper so that several identical shapes are made at the same time.
- Arranging these cut shapes to make a repeating pattern.

Doing

- The children take a piece of A4 paper and fold it in half lengthwise. They draw the outline shape of half a pot in pencil making sure the edge of the pot is along the edge of the paper so that when the pot shape is cut out the fold remains intact, and when the paper is opened the shape of the pot will be symmetrical.
- They use strips in the other colours of paper to fold them over several times before cutting the shapes for their pattern i.e. triangles, circles etc. through all the layers.
- They need to arrange these shapes to make a pattern, across or down, on their cut-out pot shape to decorate it Chulucanas style. Remind them that small shapes can be arranged on top of, and between, larger ones.
- Once they are happy with their pattern they stick it down carefully.

Display

Back the board in a neutral colour e.g. beige or cream and use thin strips of black paper to create rows of crenellated shapes (like battlements) across the board. Place a pot on each of the horizontal surfaces of the shapes. Add information about Peru and Chulucanas pottery at the bottom or beneath the display.

Mosaics

Mosaics are patterns or pictures made up of small squares of colour, usually of marble, glass, stone, terracotta etc., embedded in cement or fixative to decorate floors and walls. Mosaics have been made for thousands of years, initially by the Greeks who used water worn pebbles for their designs. The Romans learnt the art of mosaics from the Greeks, replacing pebbles with stone and glass, and used them on the walls and floors of their temples and villas, usually in the main room. Mosaics are often to be found in churches and public buildings. Similarly the Victorians used coloured patterned tiles to create complex floor designs in hallways. Mosaics are still being made throughout the world to decorate the floors and walls of modern buildings, shopping precincts etc.

Equipment Needed

Squares of black paper 21 x 21 cm approx., strips and squares of brightly coloured paper, scissors, glue, pictures of mosaics from books and the Internet.

Talk About

- Where Rome and Greece are on a map of the world.
- The design of the mosaics in the pictures plus any mosaic patterns to be found in the locality.
- Folding strips of paper before cutting shapes out of them so that several identical shapes emerge at once.
- Arranging these shapes to make a pattern, starting from the centre and working outwards.
- Leaving small gaps between each of the cut shapes so that the patterns appear similar to grouted floor and wall tiles.

Doing

- When the children have chosen their background square they choose the colours for their mosaic. The pattern will be more effective if only two or three colours are used rather than each one on offer.
- The children cut a variety of different shapes, in a range of sizes, out of the coloured paper after folding it over several times.
- They need to start in the middle of their background paper and arrange their cut shapes to make a central design. Remind them to leave a small gap between each of the shapes.
- When they are happy with their design they stick it down carefully. They cut further shapes to make a pattern around the central motif to completely fill the

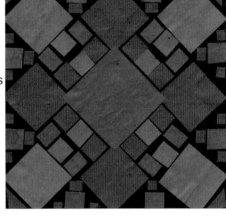

background paper. Remind them to leave a small gap between each of these shapes to get a mosaic effect, before sticking them down .

Display

Arrange pictures and information about mosaics as a block in the middle of the board. Use small coloured squares as a mosaic style border around the edge of the block. Mount the pieces of work individually and arrange them in

equally spaced rows across the board. Leave only small gaps between the pieces of work for maximum impact.

Rose Windows

Rose windows are circular stained glass windows with a central motif from which spokes radiate. They are to be found in many of the larger churches and cathedrals of Europe, particularly the Gothic ones e.g. Westminster Abbey, Notre Dame. They are made up of pieces of beautiful coloured glass joined together with lengths of lead called canes, and are thought to represent the petals of a flower opening towards the sun. The central motif is usually an image of Jesus or the Virgin Mary. Historically the rose has been the symbol of Mary the mother of Christ. The term 'rose window' probably comes from the Old French word roué, meaning wheel. In 1954 the artist Henri Matisse created a Memorial rose window in a church in New York.

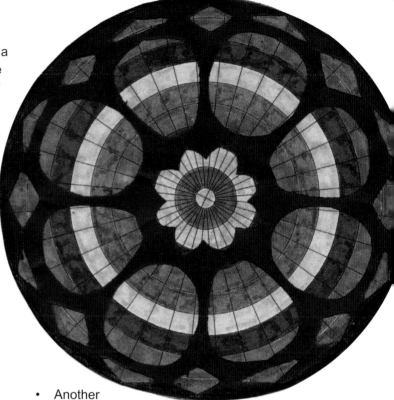

Equipment Needed

Circles of black paper approx. 19 cm diameter, polar graph paper, coloured felt-tip pens, scissors, glue, and pictures of rose windows from books and the Internet.

Talk About

- What a cathedral is and where cathedrals are found in this country.
- The colours, patterns and arrangement of stained glass in the windows.
- Adding rows of colour following the bands on the polar graph paper.
- Folding the circles of black paper several times and cutting shapes out of them along the folds (but not the edge) leaving some of the fold intact so that when the circle is opened up it is still in one piece.

Doing

- The children require a piece of polar graph paper and coloured felt tip pens. Suggest that they select only three or four colours and repeat each one several times for maximum impact. It will be easier to fill each circular band on the grid in one colour starting from the centre and working outwards.
- They take a circle of black paper and scissors, fold the circle several times, before cutting a shape out of the middle, and several shapes from along each of the folds. They open the cut circle and arrange and stick it on top of the coloured polar grid, making sure that the centre cut out shape fits over the centre of the grid. Trim off the excess around the edge.

- Another way to make such windows is to randomly colour a piece of A4 paper using felt-tip pens and then stick a cut out circular piece on top of it. Cut off the excess.
- Similar designs could be drawn using a computer graphics package - Dazzle has been used here - by first drawing a circle, adding a design of coloured dots inside it using the round brush, before 'filling' the circle with black.

Display

Arrange the completed windows in a series of circles with the title in the middle, and information and pictures about rose windows underneath.

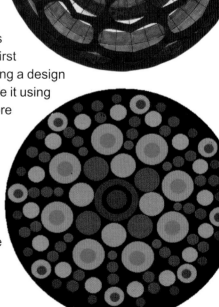

Mazes

A maze is like a puzzle to be solved. It has twists, turns, intersecting paths, blind alleys and many choices and decisions must be made to reach its centre. Mazes have appeared in the art of the Egyptians, Indians, Celts and Mediterranean people. Mazes were thought to catch and hold evil spirits and often represent the journey from darkness into light or wisdom discovered after overcoming trials. Mazes often occur in legends, the most famous of which was the lair of the Minotaur at Knossos on the island of Crete. In Medieval times mazes started to appear in churches on walls or inlaid as 'pavement mazes' on the floor for pilgrims to follow on their knees. Turf mazes and hedge mazes became very popular and were often made on a large scale, the most famous surviving historic hedge maze is that in the grounds of Hampton Court Palace in London.

Equipment Needed

Thin strips of black paper, squares of white paper 20 x 20 cm approx., scissors and glue or dot lattice grid paper, rulers and black felt tip pens or plasticene or similar modelling material and squares of white card 20 x 20 cm approx. Puzzle books that contain mazes plus pictures of actual mazes in books and from the Internet.

Talk About

- What a maze is and how to follow and negotiate a maze.
- The mazes in the puzzle books and the routes through them.
- Sticking strips of black paper to make paths in different directions.
- Drawing straight lines with a ruler and felt tip pen to join some of the dots and make paths on the dot lattice grid paper.
- Rolling the modelling material into thin sausages and then arranging them to make paths on the square of cardboard.
- Making sure there is a path that leads to the middle of the maze as well as several dead ends.

Doing

- The children decide which type of maze they are going to make and get the appropriate materials to make it.

- Before starting they need to look carefully at the layout of the mazes in the puzzle books and sketch the design for their maze in pencil on a scrap piece of paper. They may need to make several sketches before they have one to copy and use for their final piece of work.

- Finally they draw arrows that show the path through their completed maze to the centre of it.

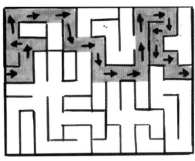

Display

Back the board in red and mount the pieces of work individually on black - the plasticene can be glued to the square of card with a strong adhesive. Put information and pictures of mazes as a block in the middle of the board plus some of the mazes from the puzzle books and arrange the individual pieces of work in equally spaced rows around it. Put further puzzle book mazes and pencils under the display to encourage interaction by the viewers.

Lace

Lace is a fabric design made up of a series of open shapes that are linked and joined by threads often in strips and used to decorate and trim clothing. These shapes are usually repeated to make up a pattern. In the Victoria and Albert Museum in London there is the oldest example of lace called mummy lace which was made in Egypt many centuries BC. Through the centuries lace making gradually spread further afield, chiefly to those countries bordering the Mediterranean Sea. It was often made by the poorest women to adorn the clothing of the rich as well as to decorate church vestments. Lace was popular as it could easily be removed from one garment and transferred to another. Countries like France, Belgium, Russia, Ireland, Spain, Hungary etc. each have their own traditional styles of lace. Lace can be made in a variety of ways, often by hand e.g. Bobbin Lace using a pillow and a series of bobbins or Needlepoint using a needle and thread or Crochet using a hook or Tatting using a shuttle though nowadays much lace is made by machine. In England, Nottingham, Bedfordshire and Devon are well known centres of lace making.

Equipment Needed

Strips of white paper, scissors, glue and circles or broad strips of black paper, white paint and fine brushes plus examples of actual lace, paper doilies, and pictures of lace from books and the Internet.

Talk About

- The countries mentioned earlier and where they can be found on a map of the world.
- The shapes that make up the lace and how they are linked and repeated to form a pattern.
- What we use lace for today and where we expect to find it.
- Folding strips of paper, cutting shapes from it whilst it is folded to produce a series of identical shapes and then arranging these shapes in a pattern.
- Drawing lines with a fine paintbrush dipped in white paint.

Doing

- The children choose a strip or circle of black paper as the background. They take strips of white paper, folding them over several times and cutting shapes through all the layers at once.
- Some strips could be folded and shapes cut out of the top and bottom of each one to form a band of repeating shapes to be used in the pattern.
- When the children have made a collection of cut shapes they need to arrange them in a repeating pattern around or along their background paper depending on its shape before sticking them down.
- Finally using a fine paintbrush and white paint they need to draw lines to link the shapes in their pattern together.

Display

Mount the individual pieces of work on black and grey and arrange them in groups of identical shapes around information about lace in the middle of the board which is backed in red.

Baskets

Baskets designed for storing and serving food and carrying goods have been made in many parts of the world since at least 2000BC. They can be made in a variety of ways (e.g. coiling, plaiting, twining and weaving) depending on the material used (e.g. grass, plant stems, leaves, reeds etc.) and on the setting in which they are made. Baskets are often intricately patterned with materials coloured with natural dyes made from tree bark, berries, leaves, clay and roots in geometric designs featuring triangles, zig-zags and diamonds. Whilst many other crafts have been mechanized no one has ever invented a machine that can make baskets and today they are still handmade. The shape and size of baskets varies from bowl shapes to bulb like shapes with or without lids depending on their purpose.

Equipment Needed

Brown paper A4 size, thin strips of coloured paper, pencils, glue, black felt tip pens, rulers, scissors, sellotape and examples of actual baskets and pictures of baskets from books and the Internet.

Talk About

- What we use baskets for today and what they are made of.
- The shape of the different baskets both real and in books and the patterns on them.
- Drawing and then cutting lines in pieces of paper that are close together but that don't reach the edge of the paper.
- Weaving by threading thin strips of paper over and under through these cut lines. Pushing the woven strips closely together and fastening them on the back of the woven piece using sellotape or glue on the front to keep them in place.

Doing

- The children take a piece of brown A4 paper, fold it in half and draw, in pencil, the outline shape of half their basket

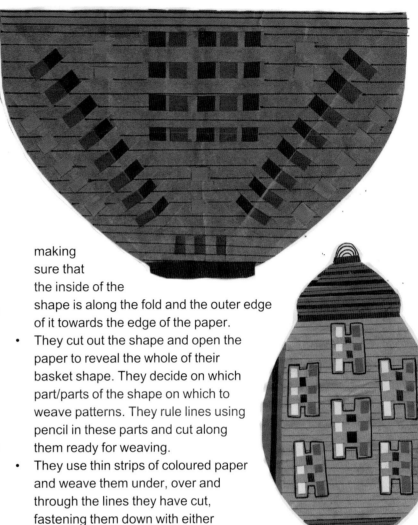

making sure that the inside of the shape is along the fold and the outer edge of it towards the edge of the paper.
- They cut out the shape and open the paper to reveal the whole of their basket shape. They decide on which part/parts of the shape on which to weave patterns. They rule lines using pencil in these parts and cut along them ready for weaving.
- They use thin strips of coloured paper and weave them under, over and through the lines they have cut, fastening them down with either sellotape on the back of the basket shape, or glue on the front.
- Lines can finally be drawn in black felt tip pen across the finished shape to make it more basket like.

Display

Put information and pictures about basket making in the middle of the board together with photographs of the children decorating their basket shapes. Arrange the completed baskets, unmounted, in rows as though they were on display for sale across the board on either side and above and below the information.

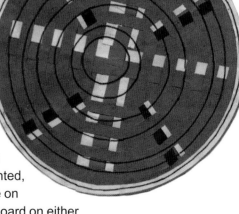

Cross Stitch Designs

Cross stitch is a form of needlework stitched onto fabric in the shape of x's. Hundreds of x shaped stitches are joined together to form a pattern or a picture. This type of embroidery has been used from early times in many communities throughout the world to decorate the sleeves and neckbands of clothes, as well as household items e.g. table linen, samplers etc. and altar cloths. Throughout Europe traditional folk embroidery often includes this stitch to add panels or a rich overall pattern to clothing, though on items for daily use only small areas are embroidered. The designs are individual to each different culture though many are similar. Symmetrical plant forms, double headed eagles, simplified figures, geometric shapes and animals are favourite motifs.

Equipment Needed

Squared maths paper cut into squares 18 x18 cm approx. or strips14 x 27 cm approx., coloured felt tip pens, pencils, scrap pieces of squared paper and actual examples of cross stitch as well as pictures from books and the Internet.

Talk About

- What cross stitch is and finding the x's on the actual examples of embroidery and those featured in pictures.

- Items on which embroidery is often found e.g. school uniform badges.
- The names of other embroidery stitches.
- Planning a design on scrap pieces of squared paper using a pencil to mark the squares to be coloured in.
- Repeating shapes within the pattern on a strip or as a border around a central motif on a square.
- Colouring in squares on the maths paper taking care to stay within the outline of each one.
- Using the same colours for matching shapes within the pattern.
- Drawing x's inside the coloured squares to make the design look more like cross stitch.

Doing

- The children plan the design of their cross stitch pattern in pencil on scrap pieces of squared paper before sketching it out on the square or strip of paper that will be their final piece of work.
- They choose the colours they are going to use to fill in their pattern. Suggest that they limit their choice to three or four to help them keep the repetition within their pattern.
- Colouring with care, they fill the squares that form their pattern, making sure they keep within the outline of each one.
- When the pattern has been coloured they add a small x to each coloured square using a black felt tip pen to make it more like cross stitch.

Display

Arrange a block of information and pictures featuring cross stitch in the middle of the board. Individually mount the pieces of work and arrange them in rows across the board and over and under the block of information. Using thin strips of black paper add a border of x's around the edge of the board.

Tie Dyeing

Tie dyeing has been practised through the ages in many countries as dyers experimented with ways of creating pattern on cloth by binding it in different ways to resist colour before dipping it in vats of dye. Different forms of tie dye are to be found in India, Japan and Africa etc. In India 'Bandhani' is the oldest tie-dye tradition still practised and involves a design made of dots in which many small points are tied with thread before the cloth is dipped in dye. Japanese tie-dye, 'Shibori', is made by stitching, folding and wrapping fabric before it is dipped in dye to produce fabric used for elaborate kimonos. African tie-dye has always been a tradition, in particular the dipping of fabric into indigo dye pits, the finished results of which are often embellished with embroidery. In the 1960s and 1970s tie-dyed clothing became popular in America and the Western world as 'flower power' and the hippie culture evolved.

Equipment Needed

White cotton fabric cut into squares approx. 20 x 20 cm, a bowl of water to wet the fabric in, a bucket for the dye mix, rubber bands, pegs, buttons, plastic money, dye e.g. Dylon Hand dye which only needs salt as a fixative, plastic lemonade bottles to store the residue of dye in and to keep it for future use, biros to write names on the individual fabric pieces before it is dyed and paper towels on which to lay the dyed fabric to dry. Pictures and examples of tie dyeing from books and the Internet.

Talk About

- What dye is and what it can be made from and the care needed to ensure it doesn't stain the clothes that the children are wearing.
- How the dye is mixed and made up following the makers instructions.
- How to fold the fabric in different

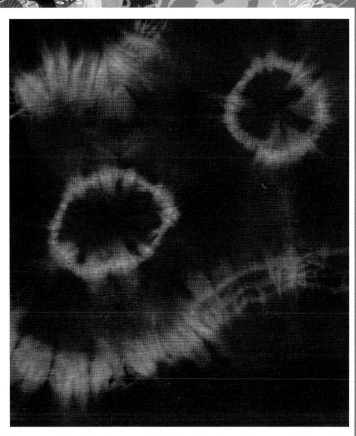

ways e.g. corner to corner, in pleats etc. and how to hold the folds together firmly with elastic bands.
- Placing buttons, beads etc. on the fabric and wrapping fabric over them and fastening them in place firmly with elastic bands.
- Writing initials on fabric in biro before it is dyed so that it can be identified.

Doing

- The children first fold, or wrap objects into their piece of fabric. They use elastic bands to hold their design in place, firmly fastened to resist the dye.
- After writing their initials on a corner of the fabric it is dampened before being placed carefully in the bucket of dye.
- After 30-40 mins the fabric can be removed from the dye (by the teacher) and rinsed under the tap before being laid on a paper towel. The children cut through the elastic bands and open the fabric to reveal their design which can then be left to dry.

Display

Ask the children to record how they made their design and display these alongside the individually mounted pieces of work around a block of pictures and information about tie-dyeing.

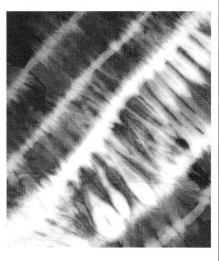

Marbling

Marbling is so called because the results look like the swirls of colour in marble stone and originated in Japan in around the twelfth century. Some believe it was discovered accidently by a member of the Japanese Imperial family who submerged ink paintings in water, watched the inks float to the surface, then put a piece of paper on the floating ink and thus preserved the image. In Turkey, India and Iran thickened water, similar to the marbling solutions of today, was used which enabled the marblers to develop detailed combed and flowing designs. During the 16th and 17th century marbling spread to Europe where bookbinders added marbled papers to the inside covers of books. Such papers are now produced by machine rather than by hand. The process of marbling is still popular and to this day the Florentines and Venetians are famous all over the world for their marbling

Equipment Needed

Marbling Inks, a shallow waterproof tray, a comb or fork to spread the ink and create patterns, vinegar (to disperse the ink) and pieces of Free art paper cut slighter smaller in size than the tray. Examples of marbled papers from books and the Internet.

Talk About

- The marbling patterns in the pictures and what they look like.
- Adding a few drops of vinegar to a shallow tray of water before using a dropper to place a few drops of marbling ink of one colour on the surface of the water.
- How to hold and squeeze a dropper both to pick up and drop the ink.
- Adding one or two other colours to the tray for a multi coloured print.
- Using a fork or comb to spread the ink and make a pattern before resting a piece of paper on top of the water to take a print.

Doing

- In turn, the children will need to pick up and drop the colours of marbling ink they want to use into the tray of water and make a pattern using a comb or fork.
- They lay a piece of paper on top of the patterned water in the tray and gently pat it all over so that all of it is coloured. Lifting it up will reveal the print.
- One or two further prints could be taken on different pieces of paper - each one will vary in density - before the next child has a turn and adds his/her choice of inks.
- The patterned paper is left to dry. Any surplus prints make excellent collage material. Marbling also looks good on coloured paper and can be done on fabric using special inks.

Display

Mount the pieces of work and fold each one as an open book before attaching them in rows across the board around a block of information about marbling.

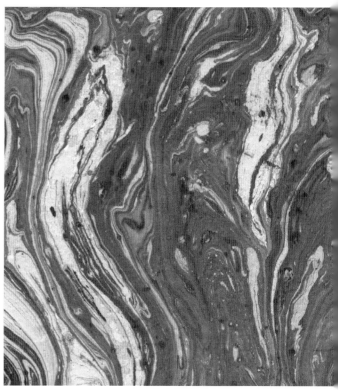